Baking Breads

GW00724487

Contents

2 **Basic rules in yeast cooking**
6 **Basic white bread**
8 **Shaping loaves** Cottage loaf; Coburg loaf; bloomer; farmhouse loaf; French stick; crescent loaf; plaited loaf
12 **Shaping rolls** Traditional round rolls; knots; twists; cottage loaves; plaits; rings; coils
14 **Enriched white bread** Three strand plait; crown loaf
16 **Short-time white bread** Garlic bread
18 **Wholemeal bread**
20 **Light brown bread** Coiled loaf; herby bread; yeast extract loaf
22 **Quick brown bread** Quick brown rolls; apricot nut bread
24 **Milk bread and rolls**
26 **Rye bread** Rye crispbread
28 **Floury baps, morning rolls and bridge rolls**
30 **Cheese bread** Cheese and celery bread; cheese and herb loaf
32 **Orange bread** Fruited orange bread; orange treacle bread; orange nut bread
34 **Currant bread and malt loaf** Spicy currant bread; fruited bread; malt bread
36 **Chelsea buns**
38 **Yorkshire tea-cakes and fruity bannock**
40 **Bath buns and Sally Lunn**
42 **Pizzas**
44 **Doughnuts** Cream; ring
46 **Iced plait** Iced fruit buns
48 **Devonshire splits** Swiss buns
50 **Hot cross buns**
52 **Lardy Cake and dough cake**
54 **Scandinavian tea ring**
56 **Danish pastries**
58 **Shaping and baking Danish pastries** Crescents; windmills and imperial stars; fruit pinwheels; cocks combs; cushions
60 **Croissants**
62 **Soda bread and scone rounds**

Basic Rules in Yeast Cooking

Freshly baked bread has a tantalizing and persistent aroma. Many people are rather scared of coping with yeast cooking although they long to produce their own bread and enjoy both the smell and satisfaction of 'baking their own'.

The baker's skill is age-old and has been handed down through the generations, but yeast cookery is really very simple provided that you follow a few simple rules and don't try to hurry. With a little practice, excellent home-made bread can be achieved.

The point to remember is that yeast is a living plant, unlike other raising agents, and in order to make it grow it needs gentle warmth, food and liquid. Given these conditions, the yeast grows rapidly and gives off a harmless and tasteless gas called carbon dioxide. These air bubbles of gas cause the dough to rise and the trapped air bubbles are then baked into the bread to give light airiness to the loaf. The yeast also produces alcohol when it is rising which gives the characteristic smell and taste to freshly baked bread.

Yeast

There are two types of yeast which can be used in breadmaking and both are readily available. Fresh yeast is often sold in health food shops and in many baker's shops which sell their own bread. Dried yeast is sold in supermarkets and chemists.

Fresh baker's yeast resembles putty and has a smell rather like wine. It will keep for up to a month in a refrigerator when stored in a loosely tied polythene bag, or for four to five days in a cool place. It will freeze for up to a year, but package it in small usable amounts, ie 15g ($\frac{1}{2}$oz) or 25g (1oz), and wrap first in cling-film and then foil.

Dried yeast will keep for up to six months if stored in an airtight container. It looks like small granules of compacted fresh yeast. Instructions for activating the yeast and quantities required are given on the tin or packet. It should either be reconstituted in warm liquid with a little sugar added and be left in a warm place until frothy (which usually takes 10–20 minutes) or it should be mixed into a flour, sugar and milk or water batter, which should be left in a warm place until frothy— about 20–30 minutes. This method is more often used for richer breads.

Basic Rules in Yeast Cooking

Flour

A strong, plain flour, called bread flour by bakers, gives the best results in breadmaking, because it has a higher gluten content than ordinary plain flour, allowing more absorption of water and thus giving a greater volume and lighter bread. A soft flour absorbs more fat but less water, thus giving a smaller volume and closer, shorter texture; but this type of flour is sometimes used for rich, fancy breads. If strong flour is not available, use an ordinary plain flour (never self-raising flour). The result will not be as successful but the recipe will still work. There are also speciality flours which are used to make certain types of bread: rye flours, stone-ground and compost-grown flours, etc. These can be incorporated into breads but they are often more expensive.

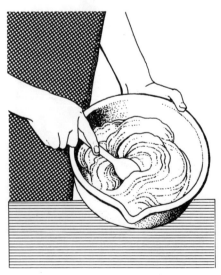

Liquid

This should be added all at once to the dough to mix it evenly. Extra flour can be easily kneaded in if the dough is too sticky, but it is not as easy to knead in extra water. The liquid is usually water or milk or a mixture of the two. Part of the liquid is used to dissolve the yeast and then the resulting yeast liquid and remaining liquid are added at the same time.

Fat

A small amount added to plain mixtures helps keep the bread moist, but it is not essential. It is usually rubbed into the dry ingredients and can be in the form of lard, butter or margarine. With richer mixtures, more fat is required and it is often melted, or sometimes softened, and added with the other liquid ingredients; sometimes it can be rubbed in. It can also be put on to the dough in flakes or spread in a softened form and then folded up and rolled out several times as with flaky pastry. This gives extra crispness and lightness by trapping the air in two ways, as is necessary in croissants and Danish pastries. Oil can be used in place of fat in some recipes.

Warmth

All yeast mixtures need warmth and, for the best results, the bowl, flour and the liquid should all be warmed before starting. Liquid needs to be between 37–43°C (98–110°F). Too much heat, or water that is too hot will quickly kill the yeast, so take care not to put a rising dough in a hot place—it just needs to be warm.

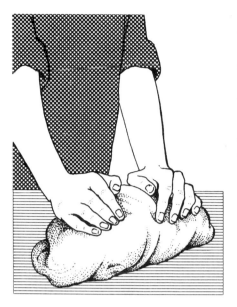

Kneading

Dough must be kneaded to strengthen and develop it in order to give a good rise. Knead by folding the dough towards you, then push down and away from you with the palm of your hand. Give the dough a quarter turn and continue the kneading process, developing a rocking action. Continue for about 10 minutes until the dough feels firm and elastic and no longer sticks to your fingers. An electric mixer can be used if the instruction book says that the mixer is suitable for kneading dough. Use a dough hook and switch on for 3–4 minutes on a low speed. Follow instructions for the maximum amount the mixer can handle. Overloading will damage the machine.

Rising

All yeast doughs must rise at least once before baking. After kneading, the dough should be shaped into a ball and put into a large covered container which has been lightly greased, eg a large oiled polythene bag, a lightly greased saucepan or a plastic storage container, etc. There must be enough space for the dough to double in size at the least.

Rising times vary with the temperature but the dough needs time to rise to double in size and should spring back when lightly pressed with a floured finger. On average, it takes $\frac{3}{4}$–1 hour in a warm place; 2 hours at room temperature; up to 12 hours in a cold room or larder, or up to 24 hours in a refrigerator. (Remember to allow refrigerated dough to return to room temperature before proceeding.) A longer, slow rise does give a stronger dough and better bread, but the type of rising should be chosen to fit in with the daily routine. Surplus dough can be stored in a polythene bag or container for up to two days in a refrigerator.

After the dough has been shaped, it is ready to be put to rise for a second time. Put the tin or baking sheet which holds the dough inside a large, oiled polythene bag or cover it with a sheet of oiled polythene to prevent a skin forming on it while it rises to double its size again. Remove the polythene before baking.

Baking

Use a hot oven, 190–230°C (375–450°F) mark 5–8. The richer, fruity mixtures are usually cooked at the lower temperature scale, with lighter breads, etc, at the hotter. A pan of hot water placed in the bottom of the oven gives the steamy atmosphere needed to bake the very best breads. Dark tins, if available, bake better bread.

Basic White Bread

The basic white loaf can be made into a variety of shapes and sizes and the following recipe can be used to make a basic dough from which other fancy breads can be made. This method of making bread can be used as a basis for all types of yeast cookery.

Ingredients

700g (1½lb) strong plain white flour
10ml (2 level tsp) salt
15g (½oz) lard
15g (½oz) fresh yeast or 7.5ml (1½ level tsp) dried yeast and 5ml (1 level tsp) caster sugar
400ml (¾pt) warm water 43°C (110°F)

Grease a 900g (2lb) loaf tin or two 450g (1lb) loaf tins or 2–3 baking sheets if you are making rolls.

Sieve the flour and salt into a bowl and then rub in the lard. Blend the fresh yeast with the water. If using dried yeast, dissolve the sugar in the water, sprinkle the yeast over the top and leave in a warm place until frothy—about 10 minutes. Add the yeast liquid to the dry ingredients all at once and mix, using a wooden spoon or fork, to form a firm dough. Add a little extra flour if necessary until the dough leaves the sides of the bowl clean. The dough should be firm but not stiff. Turn out on to a lightly floured surface and knead thoroughly until the dough is smooth and elastic and not at all sticky. To do this, hold the dough in front of you and then push it down and away from you using the palm of your hand, fold it over towards you, give a quarter turn and continue in this way for about 10 minutes. Shape it into a ball. Place the dough in a large, lightly oiled polythene bag, loosely tied at the top. This will prevent a skin forming. Put it to rise until it has doubled in size and will spring back when lightly pressed with a floured finger. For a quick rise 45–60 minutes will suffice in a warm place—about 23°C (75°F)—such as above the cooker or in an airing

cupboard. For a slower rise, about two hours will do at average room temperature. For an overnight rise, leave the dough for up to 12 hours in a cold larder or room, or up to 24 hours in a refrigerator.

All types of rising give good results, but a slow rise will give the best results. However, use whichever fits in best with your routine. Remember that refrigerated dough must be allowed to return to room temperature before proceeding. This takes about 1 hour.

Remove the risen dough from the polythene bag and turn it on to a lightly floured surface, flatten it with the knuckles to knock out the air bubbles then knead it to make it firm and ready for shaping. This takes about 2 minutes. The process is called 'knocking back'. Use flour very sparingly as too much kneaded into the dough at this stage will spoil the colour of the crust. The dough is now ready for shaping, proving and baking.

To make one large loaf, stretch the dough into an oblong shape the same width as the tin and then fold it into three and turn it over so that the seam is underneath. Smooth over the top, tuck in the ends and place it in the greased 900g (2lb) tin. For two smaller loaves, divide the dough in half and shape each piece as for the large loaf and then place in the greased 450g (1lb) loaf tins. For rolls, divide the dough into 50g (2oz) pieces and shape into rolls (see p 12). Place them well apart on greased baking sheets. Put the tins or baking sheets inside large, oiled polythene bags and put to rise again in a warm place until the dough reaches the top of the tin. This will take about 45–60 minutes. Cooler

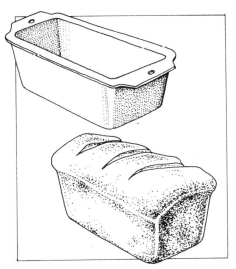

rising will take longer. Leave rolls until doubled in size. Remove the polythene and place the loaf tins on a baking sheet. Bake in a very hot oven, 230°C (450°F) mark 8, for about 40 minutes for a large loaf, about 30 minutes for smaller loaves, and 15–20 minutes for rolls. They will be well risen and golden brown. When ready, the loaves shrink slightly from the side of the tin and the base sounds hollow when tapped. Turn on to a wire rack and leave to cool.

Note The dough can be mixed and kneaded in a large electric mixer using a dough hook. But check in the instruction book on the amount of dough recommended to be made in your particular machine before you start. Overloading will cause damage. Allow about 3–4 minutes for kneading, until smooth and elastic. This bread freezes well and can be made in larger batches, if preferred.

Shaping Loaves

Once the dough is made, there are numerous ways to shape it before baking. The traditional tin loaves are easy and successful, but you can have great fun working dough into simple or exotic shapes which can be baked in a variety of tins or on baking sheets. All the following shapes can be made using the basic white bread dough.

Cottage Loaf

This traditional crusty loaf is often used as a baker's individual emblem. It is most attractive and can be made into various sized loaves or rolls.

Coburg loaf

Divide the basic white bread dough in half to make two smaller loaves or use it all for a large loaf. Remove one-third of the dough for the topknot. Shape the remainder into a bun shape and place on a greased baking sheet. Shape the smaller piece into a ball, damp the base and put it on top of the large bun. Secure by pushing your first finger and thumb right through the centre of the loaf to the base, keeping the topknot central. Brush with egg wash (see p 10), cover loosely with

oiled polythene and put to rise in a warm place until doubled in size. Remove polythene and bake in a very hot oven, 230°C (450°F) mark 8, for 30–40 minutes. For a notched cottage loaf, after proving, cut the loaf vertically with downward sweeps, using a large, sharp knife and then bake.

Coburg Loaf

Divide the basic white bread dough into two pieces and shape each piece into a round ball. To do this, roll the dough in a circular movement with the palm of your hand, gradually easing the pressure to give a smooth, round ball. Place on a baking sheet and brush all over with milk or egg wash. Mark a cross on top of the loaves using a sharp knife. Place in an oiled polythene bag and put to rise in a warm place until doubled in size then remove polythene and brush again with milk or egg wash. Bake at 230°C (450°F) mark 8 for 30–40 minutes, until golden brown. Cool on a wire rack.

Cottage loaf

Bloomer

This is a long, baton-shaped, crusty loaf with slashes all along the top. Use all the basic white bread dough for a large loaf or divide it in half for two smaller loaves. Shape each piece into an even thickness baton by rolling backwards and forwards with the palms of both hands. Tuck the ends underneath and place on a greased baking sheet. Brush with egg wash or milk, cover with a sheet of oiled polythene and put to rise in a warm place until doubled in size. Make several slashes along the top of the loaf using a sharp knife. Bake in a very hot oven, 230°C (450°F) mark 8, for 30–40 minutes, until golden brown and crusty. Cool on a wire rack. The loaves can be sprinkled with poppy seeds before baking.

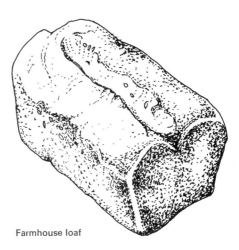

Farmhouse loaf

Farmhouse Loaf

This is an unglazed loaf which can be either baked in a tin or on a tray. It has a deep slash along the length of the loaf which opens out during baking.

Shape the dough to fit one large 900g (2lb) or two small 450g (1lb) tins and then, when proved, make a cut along the length of the loaf using a sharp knife. If you prefer a loaf baked without a tin, shape the dough into a bloomer shape, put on a greased baking sheet, cover with oiled polythene and put to rise. Before baking, make a cut along the top as for the loaves in tins. Bake in a very hot oven, 230°C (450°F) mark 8, for 30–40 minutes. To crisp up the loaves baked in tins, return them to the oven without the tins when they are cooked. Cool on a wire rack.

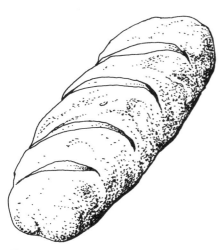

Bloomer

Shaping Loaves

French Stick

The traditional French stick is put to rise in a cloth-lined basket, but any long, narrow container or dish can be used after lining it with a well floured cloth.

Roll half the basic white bread dough out carefully, using the palms of both hands, to give a sausage shape about 35cm (14in) long. Place in the prepared container and put to rise in a warm place until it has doubled in size. Carefully turn the loaf out on to a long greased baking sheet and remove the cloth. Make diagonal cuts into the dough at 4in (10cm) intervals holding the blade of the knife horizontally. Bake in a very hot oven, 230°C (450°F) mark 8, on the centre shelf, with a bowl of boiling water on the shelf below, for 20–30 minutes. Shorter loaves can be made if preferred. For a Vienna loaf, make into thick sausage shapes with tapered ends 23–25cm (9–10in) long. Prove, slash and bake as for French sticks.

Crescent Loaf

An attractive rolled up loaf which takes a little practice to perfect. Use half the basic white bread dough and roll out to an oval shape on a well floured surface. Leave to rest for 5 minutes then roll up tightly, pulling on the edge nearest to you all the time until it forms a sausage shape. Bend into a crescent shape and place on a greased baking sheet. Cover with oiled polythene and put to rise in a warm place until the dough has doubled in size. Brush with egg wash and bake in a very hot oven, 230°C (450°F) mark 8, for 25–30 minutes, until well browned. Cool on a wire rack.

Plaited Loaf

This method of shaping can be used to make large or small plaits or rolls. Take the required amount of white bread dough and divide into three equal pieces. Roll the three pieces out to long, thin sausage shapes of equal length. Place the three strands next to each other perpendicular to you and, starting in the middle and working towards you, plait them evenly, pinching the ends tightly together. Turn the plait completely over with the plaited end away from you. Plait the remaining pieces towards you to complete the plait, and secure the ends. Place on a greased baking sheet and brush with egg wash. Cover with oiled polythene and put to rise until doubled in size. Brush again with egg wash and either leave the loaf plain or sprinkle it with poppy seeds or sesame seeds. Bake in a very hot oven, 230°C (450°F) mark 8, for 20–35 minutes, depending on size. Rolls will take 10–15 minutes. Cool on a wire rack.

Egg Wash

Beat 1 egg with 15ml (1 tbsp) water and a pinch of salt until evenly mixed.

(Opposite, from the top) French stick ; Crescent loaf ; Plaited loaf ; Brushing loaf with egg wash

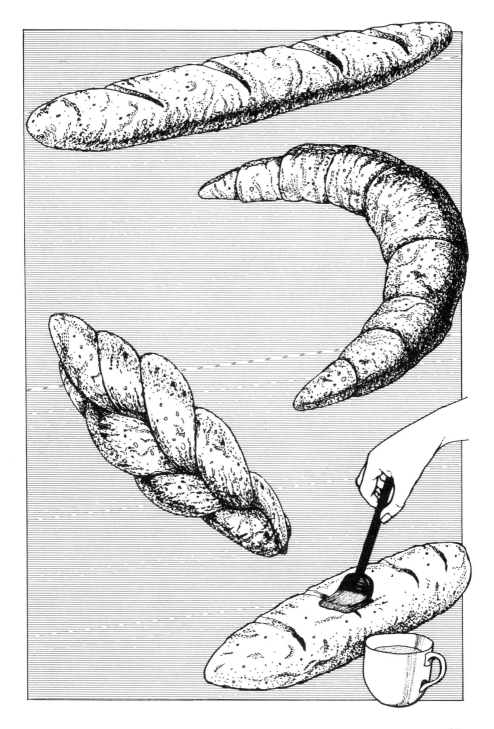

Shaping Rolls

Most doughs can be made into rolls as well as loaves. Rich, fruited doughs are best shaped into straightforward round buns, but the plainer doughs can be twisted, tied and cut into most exotic-looking rolls. The size of the rolls is up to you and dependent on the specific purpose for which they are required—but they are usually shaped from 50–75g (2–3oz) pieces of risen dough.

For soft-sided rolls—the type you pull apart—put the pieces of dough about 2cm (¾in) apart on the baking sheet, but for crusty rolls leave plenty of space around each one so that they do not touch while baking. Crustiness is helped by brushing the tops with salted water before baking.

Cover all rolls, after shaping and placing on a greased baking sheet, with a piece of oiled polythene or put the whole baking sheet into a large oiled polythene bag and put to rise in a warm place until doubled in size. This usually takes 15–30 minutes. Remove the polythene and either brush the tops with egg wash (see p 10), milk or salted water, or leave unglazed. The tops can be left plain or be sprinkled with poppy seeds, sesame seeds or, for brown rolls, cracked wheat or crushed cornflakes. Bake rolls in a very hot oven 230°C (450°F) mark 8, for 10–20 minutes, depending on size, until well risen and browned. Cool on a wire rack.

Rolls freeze well when packaged in thick-gauge polythene bags, so you can save time by baking a large batch and freezing the surplus.

Traditional Round Rolls

Divide the dough into the required sized pieces and shape each piece into a ball by rolling it round and round, on a very lightly floured surface, with the palm of your hand. Press down hard at first and gradually ease the pressure until the ball is formed. You can also shape dough into a ball by folding the edges of it into the centre until smooth, even and round, and then turning it over to keep the smooth side upwards. Place on greased baking sheets, put to rise and bake.

Knots

Roll each piece of dough into a long sausage shape with the palms of both hands and then quickly tie into a knot. With practice, double and other fancy knots can be made. Place on greased baking sheets, put to rise and bake.

Twists

Divide each piece of dough in half and shape each piece into a long, thin sausage. Twist these two pieces together, securing the ends and place on greased baking sheets. Put to rise and bake.

Cottage Loaves

Divide the dough into pieces of the required size, then break off one-third of each piece. Roll the shapes into balls and place the large balls on a greased baking sheet. Brush the tops lightly with water and put the small balls on top. Secure by pushing your first finger right through the centre to the base. Put to rise and bake.

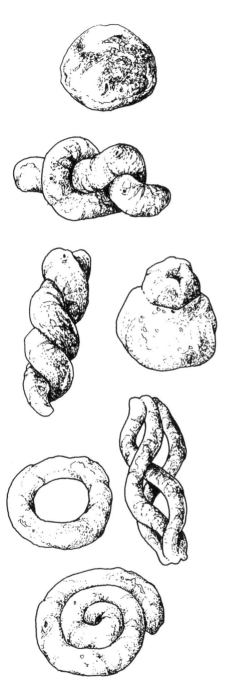

Plaits

Divide each piece of dough into three pieces and roll each out to a long, thin sausage. Plait these strands together evenly and secure the ends. The method for plaiting loaves (see p 14) gives a better shaped plait but it is not as easy to do if you are using small amounts of dough. Slightly larger pieces of dough will give a better plaited roll. Place on greased baking sheets, put to rise and bake.

Rings

Roll the pieces of dough into long, thin rolls and form into a ring. Damp the ends and mould them together securely. For twisted rings first twist two long strands of dough together and then form into a circle and mould the ends together. Place on greased baking sheets, put to rise and bake.

Coils

Roll the pieces of dough into long, thin sausage shapes. Starting at the centre, roll the sausage round and round to give a coil, tucking the ends underneath. For figure of eight coils, roll half of the dough sausage in one direction and the other half in the other direction. Place on greased baking sheets, put to rise and bake.

Enriched White Bread

This bread is made by the sponge batter method, which is especially good when using dried yeast because it does not have to be reconstituted first. It has a shorter texture than plain white bread because of the extra ingredients. Methods for making two kinds of loaves using this dough are given.

Ingredients

450g (1lb) strong plain white flour
5ml (1 level tsp) caster sugar
25g (1oz) fresh yeast or 15ml (1 level tbsp) dried yeast
250ml (8fl oz) warm milk, 143°C (110°F)
5ml (1 level tsp) salt
50g (2oz) margarine
1 egg, beaten

Glaze

1 egg, beaten
5ml (1 level tsp) caster sugar
15ml (1tbsp) water
Poppy seeds (optional)

Put 150g (5oz) sieved flour into a bowl with the sugar, yeast (either fresh or dried) and the milk. Put aside in a warm place for about 20 minutes until it is frothy and the yeast dissolved. Sieve the remaining flour with the salt into a bowl and rub in the margarine until the mixture resembles fine breadcrumbs. Add the beaten egg and the flour mixture to the yeast batter and mix well to give a fairly soft dough which will leave the sides of the bowl clean.

Turn the dough on to a lightly floured surface and knead (see p 5) until it is smooth and no longer sticky.

This should take about 10 minutes by hand or 3–4 minutes if you are using an electric mixer (no extra flour should be necessary). Form the dough into a ball and place in a lightly oiled polythene bag, tie loosely and put to rise in a warm place until doubled in size. See p 5 for alternate rising times.

Remove the dough from the polythene bag on to a sparsely floured surface and knead lightly. Divide the dough into two pieces ready for shaping into plaits.

Three Strand Plait

Divide each piece of dough into three, then roll each piece into a strand of about 30cm (12in). Lay the three strands side-by-side on a flat surface. Beginning in the middle, plait the three strands towards you, pinching the ends together. Turn the plait completely over so that the unplaited strands are perpendicular to you ; then plait these to complete the loaf, pinching the ends together. Place on a greased baking sheet.

Crown Loaf

Grease one 22.5cm (9in) or two 15cm (6in) round sandwich tins. Divide all the dough into twelve equal-sized pieces and roll each piece into a ball. Place these in a circle round the edge of the large tin with three or four in the middle or, if you are using the smaller tins, five round the edge of each one, with one ball in the centre.
For each loaf continue as follows:

Combine the beaten egg, sugar and water for the glaze and brush all over the plait or crowns. Sprinkle with poppy seeds or sesame seeds, if liked.

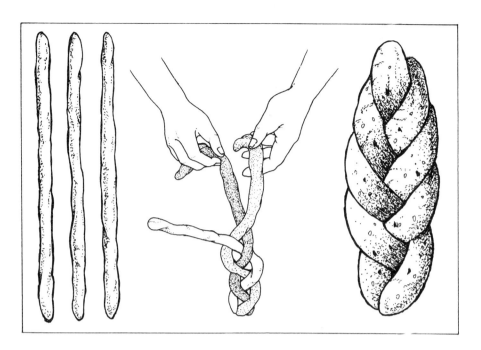

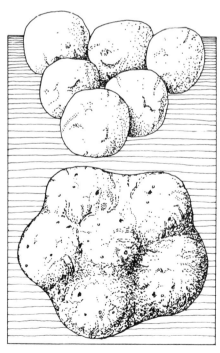

Put to rise inside a lightly oiled polythene bag in a warm place until the dough has doubled in size.

Bake in a moderately hot oven, 190 °C (375 °F) mark 5, for 45–50 minutes for the plaits, 50–60 minutes for the large crown, or 35–40 minutes for the small crowns, until they are lightly browned and hollow sounding when tapped on the base. Cool on a wire rack.

This dough can also be used for making rolls (see p 12 for shaping and baking).

Short-time White Bread

This recipe cuts out the initial rising stage of breadmaking and replaces it with a 5–10 minute rest period. The ascorbic acid (Vitamin C) used is available from larger chemists in 25, 50 or 100mg tablet form and it is crushed and added to the dry ingredients in the liquid. Fresh yeast only should be used in this recipe.

Ingredients

700g (1½lb) strong plain white flour
10ml (2 level tsp) salt
5ml (1 level tsp) caster sugar
25g (1oz) lard or margarine
25g (1oz) fresh yeast
400ml (14fl oz) warm water 43°C
   (110°F)
25mg ascorbic acid, crushed

Sieve the flour, salt and sugar into a bowl. Rub in the lard or margarine. Blend the yeast in the water and then add the crushed ascorbic acid. Add the yeast liquid to the dry ingredients all at once and mix to form a firm dough which will leave the sides of the bowl clean. Add a little extra flour, if necessary. Turn the dough on to a lightly floured surface and knead thoroughly until smooth, firm and elastic—this should take about 10 minutes by hand or 3–4 minutes if you are using an electric mixer. Form into a ball, put into a lightly oiled polythene bag and tie loosely. Leave to rest for 5 minutes. Remove the dough from the bag and knead lightly ready for shaping.

For a large loaf, shape to fit a greased 900g (2lb) loaf tin. Stretch the dough into an oblong shape the same width as the tin, fold into three, then turn it

over so that the seam is underneath. Smooth the top, tuck in the ends and place in the tin.

For two smaller loaves, shape as above to fit 2 greased 450g (1 lb) loaf tins. For other shaped loaves, see p 8.

This dough can also be used to make eighteen to twenty plain or shaped rolls (see p 12) : put on to greased baking sheets about 2.5cm (1 in) apart. Place the tins inside an oiled polythene bag or cover the rolls with a sheet of polythene and put to rise until doubled in size. The dough should spring back when lightly pressed with a floured finger. Rising should take 45–60 minutes at room temperature for loaves and up to 30 minutes for rolls. Remove the polythene and either leave plain, dust with flour or brush lightly with milk or beaten egg. Bake in a very hot oven, 230°C (450°F)

mark 8, for 30–35 minutes for the large loaf, 25–30 minutes for the smaller loaves, and 15–20 minutes for rolls, until well risen and golden brown. Turn out on to a wire rack to cool. For a crisper crust return the loaf to the oven for 4–5 minutes without the tin.

Garlic Bread

The above recipe is ideal for garlic bread if the loaves are shaped into batons or sticks. Beat 100–150g (4–6oz) butter until smooth and add several crushed cloves of garlic to taste. Cut the bread into slanting slices 2.5cm (1 in) thick, but try not to sever the slices right through the loaf (the ideal is to leave the bread intact all the way along the bottom). Put the bread on to a piece of foil large enough to enclose it. Then spread the butter paste down into each slice on both sides. Wrap the foil round the bread and put in a medium to hot oven for about 15 minutes. After ten minutes open the foil parcel a little to make the bread a crisp golden brown.

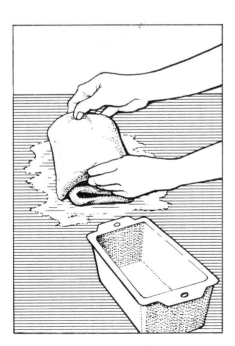

Wholemeal Bread

This bread can be made with any of the plain brown-bread flours whether stone-ground or compost grown, etc.

Ingredients

50g (2oz) fresh yeast or 30ml (2 level tbsp) dried yeast and 5ml (1 level tsp) caster sugar
900ml (1½pt) warm water
1.4kg (3lb) plain wholemeal flour
30ml (2 level tbsp) caster sugar
10–20ml (2–4 level tsp) salt
25g (1oz) lard

Blend the fresh yeast with one-third of the water. For dried yeast, dissolve the 5ml (1 tsp) sugar in one-third of the water, sprinkle over the dried yeast and leave in a warm place until frothy—about 10 minutes.

Mix the flour, sugar and salt together in a bowl and rub in the lard. Stir the yeast liquid into the dry ingredients with sufficient of the remaining water to form a firm dough which leaves the sides of the bowl clean.

Turn out on to a lightly floured surface and knead the dough until firm, smooth, elastic and no longer sticky. This should take about 10 minutes by hand or 3–4 minutes if you are using an electric mixer and dough hook. (This amount of dough will be too large to be kneaded all at once in a mixer, so do it in two halves to prevent overloading.) Shape the dough into a ball and put it into a lightly oiled poylthene bag. Tie the bag loosely and put it to rise in a warm place until the dough has doubled in size—this should take about 1 hour (see p 5 for alternate rising times).

Turn the dough out on to a lightly floured surface, knock back and knead again until smooth. Divide into two or four pieces and shape to fit two greased 900g (2lb) loaf tins or four 450g (1lb) tins (see p 8 for method of shaping). Brush the tops of the loaves with salted water and put each one in a warm place to rise in a lightly greased polythene bag, until the dough reaches the top of the tins—about 1 hour. Bake in a very hot oven, 230°C (450°F) mark 8, for 30–40 minutes, depending on the size of the loaves, until well risen, with the base sounding hollow when turned out and tapped. Cool on a wire rack.

Alternate Shapings

Shape each quarter of the dough into a round cob and place on greased baking sheets. Either dust with flour or brush with salted water and sprinkle with cracked wheat. Put to rise and bake as above.
Shape all the dough into a large, round cob or halve the dough and form into two smaller cobs and place on greased baking sheets. Using a sharp knife, score each cob deeply into four quarters and sprinkle with cracked wheat or flour. Put to rise as above. Before baking, again mark into quarters and bake for 30–45 minutes depending on size. Cool on a wire rack and break into quarters to serve.

Divide the dough into two or four pieces, then divide each piece again into four. Shape into rolls. Place side-by-side in the appropriate sized greased loaf tins. Put to rise and bake as above.

Note Any of the shapings described on p 8 for loaves or p 12 for rolls can be used for this dough. For crusty brown bread or rolls, brush the tops with salt water after shaping. Cracked wheat or crushed cornflakes can be sprinkled over the top.

Light Brown Bread

This loaf has only a small proportion of brown flour, but it does give colour and flavour to a light loaf with a floury top. It also keeps fresh for longer than pure wholemeal breads.

Ingredients

450g (1lb) strong plain white flour
7.5ml (1½ level tsp) salt
225g (½lb) plain wholemeal flour
25g (1oz) lard or margarine
25g (1oz) fresh yeast or 15ml (1 level
    tbsp) dried yeast and 5ml (1 level
    tsp) caster sugar
450g (¾pt) warm water 43°C (110°F)

Sieve the white flour and salt into a bowl. Add the wholemeal flour and mix thoroughly. Rub the lard into the dry ingredients. Blend the fresh yeast in half of the water. If using dried yeast, dissolve the 5ml (1 tsp) sugar in half of the water, sprinkle the dried yeast over the top and leave in a warm place until frothy—about 10 minutes. Add the yeast liquid and remaining water to the dry ingredients and mix to form a fairly firm dough which leaves the sides of the bowl clean. Turn out on to a floured surface and knead the dough until smooth, elastic and no longer sticky. This should take about 10 minutes by hand or 3–4 minutes if you are using an electric mixer.

Shape the dough into a ball, place in an oiled polythene bag and secure the top. Put to rise in a warm place for about 1 hour or until it has doubled in size and it springs back when pressed lightly with a floured finger. Other rising times to remember are 2 hours at room temperature, up to 12 hours in a cold larder or up to 24 hours in a refrigerator. Remember to allow refrigerated dough to return to room temperature before shaping. This takes about 1 hour.

Remove the dough from the polythene, knock back and knead for about 2 minutes until smooth and ready for shaping. This dough can be used for one large loaf using a greased 900g (2lb) loaf tin, for two smaller loaves using two 450g (1lb) tins, for any of the loaf shapes described on pp 8–11, or for any of the rolls described on p 12. It is also good for making into flat bap rolls (see p 28) which should be dusted with flour before baking.

Coiled Loaf

Grease a deep pie tin about 17.5cm (7in) in diameter. Use half the dough and roll this into a long, thin sausage about 4cm (1½in) thick. Starting at the outside edge of the tin, wind the sausage of dough in to the centre of the tin with the centre being raised up higher than the outside. Loaves and rolls can be dusted with flour or brushed with salt water, milk or beaten egg before proving, and can be sprinkled with cracked wheat or crushed cornflakes if liked.

Variations

Herby Bread

At the knocking-back stage, knead in 45–60ml (3–4tbsp) chopped mixed herbs and a little powdered garlic, if liked. Continue as for basic light brown bread for loaves or rolls.

Yeast Extract Loaf

Stretch out the knocked-back dough ready to fold to fit the tins, then spread evenly over it 15–30ml (1–2 tbsp) yeast extract. Fold up and place in the prepared tin. Continue as for basic light brown bread.

Quick Brown Bread

This is an easy recipe which requires only one rise. The texture is a little closer than traditional home-baked bread and it may not stay fresh quite as long, but it is well worth making for the amount of time it saves.

Ingredients

15g ($\frac{1}{2}$oz) fresh yeast or 10ml (2 level tsp) dried yeast and 5ml (1 level tsp) caster sugar
Approx 300ml (approx $\frac{1}{2}$pt) warm water 43°C (110°F)
450g (1lb) plain wholemeal flour or 225g ($\frac{1}{2}$lb) each plain wholemeal flour and strong plain white flour
5ml (1 level tsp) caster sugar
7.5ml (1$\frac{1}{2}$ level tsp) salt
25g (1oz) lard

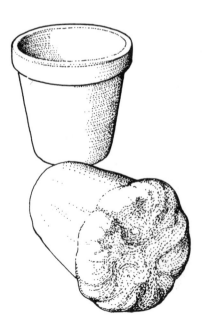

Blend the fresh yeast with the water. For dried yeast, dissolve the 5ml (1tsp) sugar in half the water, sprinkle the dried yeast over the top and leave in a warm place until frothy—about 10 minutes. Mix together the flour(s), sugar and salt in a bowl and rub in the lard.

Add the yeast liquid and remaining water to the dry ingredients and mix to a fairly soft dough, adding more warm water if necessary. Turn the dough on to a lightly floured surface and knead (see p 5) until smooth, elastic and no longer sticky—about 10 minutes by hand or 3–4 minutes if you are using an electric mixer. Divide the dough into two equal pieces. Shape the dough to fit two 450g (1lb) greased loaf tins or shape into two round cobs and place on a greased baking sheet.

Alternatively, you can make flower-pot loaves. Use two clean 10–12cm (4–5in) terracotta flower-pots and grease well. Bake the empty pots in a hot oven for about 20 minutes, and repeat this several times before filling them with dough; this will prevent the loaves from sticking. Shape each piece of dough to half-fill a flower-pot. Brush the tops with salt water and sprinkle with cracked wheat or crushed cornflakes.

Place the tins in oiled polythene bags and put to rise in a warm place for about 1 hour or until doubled in size. The dough should spring back when pressed with a floured finger. (For alternate rising times see p 5.)
Remove the tins from the polythene and bake in a very hot oven, 230°C (450°F) mark 8, for 15 minutes. Reduce the temperature to fairly hot, 200°C (400°F) mark 6, for a further 30–40

minutes for loaves, or 20–30 minutes for cobs. Cook flower-pots in a very hot oven for about 40 minutes. Turn out and cool on a wire rack.

Quick Brown Rolls

The dough from the above recipe can also be used for shaping into rolls:

Divide the dough into twelve pieces and roll into rounds. Place on greased or floured baking sheets. Leave plain or mark with a cross.

You can also shape into twelve finger rolls and put them on to greased or floured baking sheets. For soft-sided rolls, place $\frac{3}{4}$cm ($\frac{1}{4}$in) apart and dredge with flour; for crusty rolls, place well apart and brush with salt water. A third method is to flatten the dough to 1.5cm ($\frac{1}{2}$in) thickness and cut it into rounds using a 6cm ($2\frac{1}{2}$in) cutter. Place on greased or floured baking sheets.

Cover the rolls with oiled polythene and put to rise in a warm place until doubled in size. Bake in a very hot oven, 230°C (450°F) mark 8, for 20–25 minutes, until well risen and browned. Cool on a wire rack. Do not pull the soft-sided rolls apart until cold.

Variation

Apricot Nut Bread

Using the above recipe and half brown and half white flour, add the grated rind of 1 lemon, 100g (4oz) chopped shelled nuts and 225g (8oz) chopped dried apricots to the rubbed in ingredients before adding the yeast liquid. Continue as above, shape to fit two 450g (1lb) greased loaf tins. Prove and bake as above. Brush the hot cooked loaf with a wet pastry brush dipped in honey or syrup.

Milk Bread and Rolls

This bread can be made using either all milk or half milk and half water. Using milk only gives a close textured loaf with a softer crust.

Ingredients

15g ($\frac{1}{2}$oz) fresh yeast or 7.5ml (1$\frac{1}{2}$ level tsp) dried yeast and 5ml (1 level tsp) caster sugar
Approx 400ml (approx $\frac{3}{4}$pt) warm milk or milk and water mixed, 43°C (110°F)
700g (1$\frac{1}{2}$lb) strong plain white flour
10ml (2 level tsp) salt
50g (2oz) lard or margarine

Blend the fresh yeast with the milk. For dried yeast, dissolve the sugar in 150ml ($\frac{1}{4}$pt) milk, then sprinkle the dried yeast over the top and leave until frothy. This takes about 10 minutes in a warm place.

Sieve the flour and salt into a bowl and rub in the fat. Add the yeast liquid and remaining milk and mix to a fairly soft dough, adding a little more warm milk, if necessary. Turn out on to a floured surface and knead until smooth and elastic—about 10 minutes by hand or 3–4 minutes if you are using an electric mixer. Shape into a ball and place in a lightly oiled polythene bag. Tie the top loosely and put to rise until doubled in size. The dough should spring back when pressed lightly with a floured finger. Allow 45–60 minutes in a warm place, 2 hours at average room temperature, up to 12 hours in a cold larder or up to 24 hours in a refrigerator. (Refrigerated dough must be allowed to return to room temperature before shaping. This takes about 1 hour.) Remove the dough from the polythene, knock back and knead until smooth and ready for shaping.

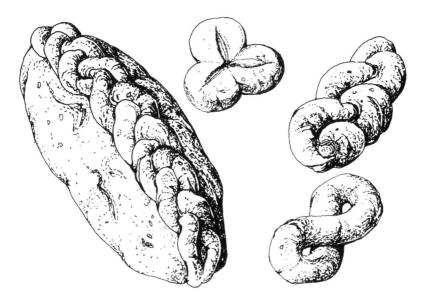

Loaves

Shape the dough to fit a greased 900g (2lb) loaf tin or two 450g (1lb) tins or make into any of the shapes described on pp 8–11.

Decorated Baton

Break off a quarter of the dough and divide this small amount into two equal pieces. Shape the remaining dough into a fat baton shape, slightly tapering at the ends, and place on a greased baking sheet. Roll each of the small pieces of dough into long sausages and twist lightly together. Brush the top of the baton with water and lay the twist on top, folding the ends under the loaf. Sprinkle lightly with poppy seeds, if liked.

Put the loaves inside an oiled polythene bag and put to rise for about 1 hour at room temperature. Brush the loaves with beaten egg or milk, or dust with flour. Bake in a hot oven, 220°C (425°F) mark 7, for 30–40 minutes.

Rolls

Divide the dough into 50g (2oz) pieces and shape into rolls. Place on greased baking sheets. Popular shapes for rolls are twists, plaits, cottage loaves, knots, rings, figures of eight, etc (see pp 12–13 for methods of shaping).

Cover the rolls with a sheet of oiled polythene and put to rise until the dough doubles in size, about 15–20 minutes at room temperature. They can be brushed with beaten egg or milk, or dusted with flour before baking, if liked. Cook in a hot oven, 220°C (425°F) mark 7, for 15–20 minutes. Cool on a wire rack.

Note This bread freezes well.

Rye Bread

Many people like rye bread and want to make their own version. It does, however, take longer than most breads as it requires a starter (or sour) dough. This needs to be made up and left for 12–24 hours before you can actually make the bread. However, the finished loaf is worth the trouble.

Ingredients

Starter Dough

150g (5oz) coarse rye flour
150g (5oz) fine rye flour
150ml ($\frac{1}{4}$pt) sour milk
5ml (1 level tsp) caster sugar.

Second Dough

125ml (scant $\frac{1}{4}$pt) warm water, 43°C (110°F)
15ml (1 tbsp) black treacle
25g (1oz) fresh yeast or 15ml (1 level tbsp) dried yeast
300g (10oz) strong plain white flour
15g ($\frac{1}{2}$oz) salt

Starch Glaze

10ml (2 level tsp) cornflour
Approx 100ml (approx 4fl oz) water

Make the starter dough by mixing all the ingredients together in a bowl. Leave them overnight or up to 24 hours in a covered bowl in a cool place. The next day mix the warm water and treacle together in a large bowl and either crumble in the fresh yeast or sprinkle in the dried yeast together with 30ml (2tbsp) of flour. Leave the mixture in a warm place until frothy—about 10 minutes. Sieve the rest of the flour together with the salt into a bowl and add to the yeast batter together with the starter dough. Mix the whole to give a firm but slightly sticky dough. Turn on to a floured surface and knead well for about 5–10 minutes until smooth and firm. Shape into a ball, place in an oiled polythene bag and put to rise in a warm place for 1–1$\frac{1}{2}$ hours or until doubled in size.

Turn out on to a floured surface, knock back the dough and knead until smooth. Divide into two pieces and shape either into a cob (a round ball) or into a baton (a thick fat sausage shape) and place on greased baking sheets. Cover with a sheet of oiled polythene and put to rise in a warm place until the dough has doubled in size and springs back when pressed lightly with a floured finger.

Make the starch glaze by blending the cornflour in a little cold water and adding sufficient boiling water. Stir continuously until the glaze clears. It should give about 100ml (4fl oz). Cool the glaze.

Remove the polythene and brush the loaves with the cooled starch glaze. Preheat the oven to very hot, 230°C (450°F) mark 8. Reduce to fairly hot,

200°C (400°F) mark 6, and put the loaves in the centre of the oven and bake for 30 minutes. Reduce the heat to 150°C (300°F) mark 2, and brush the loaves again with glaze. Bake for a further 30 minutes, glaze again and return to the oven for 1–2 minutes. Remove to a wire rack to cool.

Note For a coarser-textured loaf, use half fine rye flour and half strong white flour in place of all white flour in the second dough.

Rye Crispbread

Ingredients

450g (1lb) risen rye bread dough (see p 26)
50g (2oz) lard or 30ml (2 tbsp) oil
10ml (2 level tsp) salt
15ml (1 tbsp) coarse rye or crushed cornflakes

Place the dough in a bowl and add either the lard, cut into small pieces, or the oil, the salt and rye or cornflakes. Knead and squeeze all the ingredients together until evenly blended. Roll the dough out thinly on a floured surface and place on greased baking sheets. Cut the dough into squares or rectangles using either a pastry wheel or a sharp knife. Cover with a sheet of oiled polythene and put to rise in a warm place until puffy. Bake in a fairly hot oven, 200°C (400°F) mark 6, for about 15 minutes, then turn off the heat and crisp off in the cooling oven. Remove to a wire rack and leave to cool. Store in an airtight container.

Floury Baps, Morning Rolls and Bridge Rolls

Floury Baps and Morning Rolls

Baps are the traditional flat loaves of Scotland. The small baps are known as morning rolls and were at one time served exclusively at breakfast. The rolls are particularly good when served warm.

Ingredients

15g (½oz) fresh yeast or 10ml (2 level
   tsp) dried yeast and 2.5ml (½ level
   tsp) caster sugar
300ml (½pt) warm milk and water
   mixed, 43°C (110°F)
450g (1lb) strong plain white flour
5ml (1 level tsp) salt
50g (2oz) lard or white vegetable fat

Blend the fresh yeast with the warm liquid. If you are using dried yeast, dissolve the 2.5ml (½tsp) caster sugar in half the warm liquid, add the dried yeast, sprinkling it over the top and leave in a warm place until frothy—about 10 minutes.

Sieve the flour and salt into a bowl, then rub in the fat. Stir the yeast liquid and the remaining liquid all at once into the dry ingredients and mix to form a softish dough, adding a little extra flour if necessary to leave the sides of the bowl clean. Turn out on to a lightly floured surface and knead the dough until smooth and elastic. This will take about 5 minutes by hand or 2–3 minutes if you are using an electric mixer. Shape the dough into a ball and place in a lightly oiled polythene bag. Tie loosely and put to rise in a warm

place until doubled in size (see p 5 for alternate rising times). Turn the dough out on to a lightly floured surface, knock back and knead until smooth and firm.

Use half the dough to make the large bap; shape into a ball and, using a floured rolling-pin, roll out into a round about 2cm (¾in) thick. Place on a floured baking sheet and dredge the

top with flour. Divide the remaining dough into five or six pieces; roll each piece into a ball and then roll out to an oval about 1.5cm (½in) thick. Place on the floured baking sheet and dredge with flour.

Cover lightly with a sheet of oiled polythene and put to rise at room temperature for about 45 minutes or until doubled in size. Remove the polythene and press the bap and rolls gently in the centre with three fingers to prevent blisters forming during cooking. Bake in the centre of a fairly hot oven, 200°C (400°F) mark 6, for 20–30 minutes for the bap and 15–20 minutes for the rolls until they turn a pale golden brown. Cool on a wire rack. This recipe makes two large baps or twelve morning rolls, or one bap and six morning rolls.

Note Small brown baps can be made using the light brown bread recipe on p 20. This bread and the rolls freeze well.

Bridge Rolls

These are the traditional rolls used for parties, buffets, etc either to be filled and left whole or to be cut in half and served as two open rolls.

Ingredients

15g (½oz) fresh yeast or 7.5ml (1½ level tsp) dried yeast and 5ml (1 level tsp) caster sugar
100ml (4fl oz) warm milk, 43°C (110°F)
225g (8oz) plain white flour
5ml (1 level tsp) salt
50g (2oz) butter or margarine
1 egg, beaten
1 beaten egg to glaze

Blend the fresh yeast with the warm milk. For dried yeast dissolve the sugar in the milk, sprinkle the dried yeast over the top and leave in a warm place until frothy—about 10 minutes. Sieve the flour and salt into a bowl and rub in the fat until the mixture resembles fine breadcrumbs. Add the yeast liquid and beaten egg to the dry ingredients and mix to form a fairly soft dough, adding a little extra milk or flour, if necessary. Beat the mixture well, then turn on to a floured surface and knead well until smooth and elastic. Place in a lightly greased polythene bag or replace in the bowl and cover securely with oiled polythene and put to rise until doubled in size. This should take about 1 hour in a warm place (see p 5 for alternate rising times). Turn the dough out on to a floured surface and knead lightly until smooth and ready for shaping. The rolls can be made into various sizes, so divide the dough into the required amounts, ie 25g (1oz), 40g (1½oz), 50g (2oz), or larger or smaller if so required. Shape each piece of dough into a roll or finger shape with slightly tapering ends by pressing down and rolling backwards and forwards with the palm of either one hand or two, depending on the size of the roll, until the required shape and size is achieved. Place on greased baking sheets in rows fairly close together. They will expand to just touch during baking. For soft-sided rolls, place the dough shapes ¾cm (¼in) apart so that they really stick together during baking. Cover with a sheet of oiled polythene and put to rise for 15–20 minutes or until doubled in size. The rolls can be brushed with beaten egg before baking to give the traditional glazed top of bridge rolls. Bake in a hot oven, 220°C (425°F) mark 8, for 10–20 minutes depending on size, until golden brown. Slide them on to a wire rack and leave them joined together until cold.

Note These rolls freeze well. For larger quantities of bridge rolls, double the quantities of the ingredients.

Cheese Bread

A delicious flavoured loaf with a cheesy crust. It is ideal for something a little different for sandwiches, picnics and toasted dishes.

Ingredients

450g (1lb) strong plain white flour
10ml (2 level tsp) salt
5ml (1 level tsp) dry mustard
Ground pepper to taste
100–150g (4–6oz) Cheddar cheese, finely grated
15g ($\frac{1}{2}$oz) fresh yeast or 10ml (2 level tsp) dried yeast and 5ml (1 level tsp) caster sugar
300ml ($\frac{1}{2}$pt) warm water, 43°C (110°F)

In a large bowl sieve together the flour, salt, mustard and pepper. Mix in most of the cheese, reserving a little to sprinkle on top of the loaves. Blend the fresh yeast with the warm liquid. For dried yeast, dissolve the sugar in the liquid then sprinkle the dried yeast over the top and leave in a warm place until frothy—about 10 minutes. Add the yeast liquid to the dry ingredients and mix to form a firm dough, adding a little extra flour, if necessary, to leave the sides of the bowl clean.

Turn out on to a lightly floured surface and knead until smooth and elastic and no longer sticky—about 10 minutes by hand or 3–4 minutes if you are using an electric mixer. Shape into a ball and put into a lightly oiled polythene bag. Put to rise in a warm place for about 1 hour or until doubled in size. The dough should spring back when lightly pressed with a floured finger (see p 5 for alternate rising times).

Turn the dough out on to a lightly floured surface, knock back and knead until smooth and ready for shaping. Either shape to fit a greased 900g (2lb) loaf tin or two 450g (1lb) loaf tins, or shape into one or more of the loaves described on pp 8–11. The dough can also be used to make twelve to fourteen rolls (for shaping see p 12).

Put the loaves inside a large oiled polythene bag and put to rise in a warm place until the dough reaches the top of the tins—about 45 minutes. Cover the rolls with oiled polythene and put to rise until they have doubled in size. Remove the polythene, sprinkle the remaining grated cheese over the loaves or rolls and bake in a moderately hot oven 190°C (375°F) mark 5, allowing about 45 minutes for loaves or 20 minutes for rolls. Take care not to overbake or overbrown. Cool on a wire rack.

Variations

Cheese and Celery Bread

Mix 25g (1oz) grated cheese with 5ml (1 level tsp) celery salt and sprinkle over the loaf before baking.

Cheese and Herb Loaf

At the knock back stage of making the bread, knead 45–60ml (3–4 tbsp) freshly chopped herbs (or half the quantity if using dried herbs) into the dough. Use either mixed herbs or one particular herb of your choice. Continue as for cheese bread.

Note. This bread freezes well.

Orange Bread

This bread has a very pleasant, if unusual, flavour. It is especially good when eaten with cream cheese, chocolate spread or marmalade, and also toasts well. It is made from the hulls of oranges after the juice has been squeezed out, so it makes use of something usually thrown away.

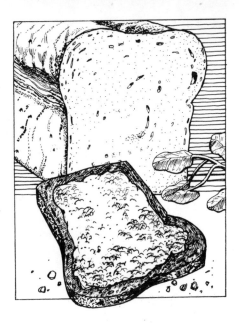

Ingredients

450g (1lb) strong plain white flour
10ml (2 level tsp) salt
25g (1oz) caster sugar
25g (1oz) fresh yeast or 15ml (1 level tbsp) dried yeast and 5ml (1 level tsp) caster sugar
150ml ($\frac{1}{4}$pt) warm water, 43°C (110°F)
1 egg, beaten
3 medium or 2 large shells (ie halves) of orange

Orange pulp

Either mince or very finely chop the peel shells from oranges which have had the juice squeezed out or, if preferred, use one whole orange minced.

Sieve the flour and salt into a bowl and mix in the sugar. Dissolve the fresh yeast in the water or, for dried yeast, dissolve 5ml (1 tsp) sugar in the water, sprinkle the dried yeast over the top and leave in a warm place until frothy—about 10 minutes. Add the yeast liquid to the dry ingredients together with the egg and orange pulp and mix to form a softish dough, adding a little extra flour if necessary.

Turn on to a floured surface and knead until smooth and firm—about 10 minutes by hand or 3–4 minutes if you are using an electric mixer. Shape into a ball, place in a lightly oiled polythene bag and tie the end. Put to rise in a warm place for about 1 hour or until doubled in size and the dough springs back when pressed lightly with a floured finger (see p 5 for alternate rising times). Turn the dough out on to a lightly floured surface, knock back and knead lightly until smooth—about 2 minutes.

Either shape to fit a greased 900g (2lb) loaf tin for a large loaf or, for small loaves, use two 450g (1lb) loaf tins. For a farmhouse-shaped loaf, score right along the top of the loaf crust. Put the tins inside an oiled polythene bag and put to rise in a warm place until the dough reaches the top of the tins. Remove the polythene and bake in a fairly hot oven, 200°C (400°F) mark 6, for 40–50 minutes for a large loaf or 30–35 minutes for small loaves, until well browned and the base sounds hollow when tapped. Turn out on to a wire rack and brush the crust of the loaf immediately with a wet pastry brush dipped in honey or syrup or with melted butter. Leave to cool.

Variations

Fruited Orange Bread

Add 175g (6oz) mixed dried fruit to the dry ingredients before adding the liquid and then proceed as for basic orange bread.

Orange Treacle Bread

450g (1lb) risen orange bread dough (ie half the basic recipe)
60ml (4tbsp) black treacle

Before shaping, put the risen dough into a bowl and add the treacle. Squeeze and knead the dough until the treacle is evenly mixed and is no longer sticky. Pour into a greased 450g (1lb) loaf tin, cover with oiled polythene and put to rise. Proceed as for basic orange bread.

Orange Nut Bread

450g (1lb) risen orange bread dough (ie half basic recipe)
100g (4oz) shelled walnuts, chopped
30ml (2tbsp) thick honey

Put the risen dough before shaping into a bowl and add the walnuts and honey. Squeeze and knead the dough until evenly mixed, then transfer to a greased 450g (1lb) loaf tin. Cover with oiled polythene and put to rise. Proceed as for basic orange bread.

Currant Bread and Malt Loaf

Currant Bread

Ingredients

450g (1 lb) strong plain white flour
5ml (1 level tsp) salt
25g (1 oz) caster sugar
25g (1 oz) butter or margarine
100g (4oz) currants
25g (1 oz) fresh yeast or 15ml (1 level tbsp) dried yeast and 5ml (1 level tsp) caster sugar
300ml ($\frac{1}{2}$pt) warm milk and water mixed, 43°C (110°F)
Honey or syrup to glaze

Sieve the flour and salt into a bowl. Mix in the sugar and then rub in the fat until the mixture resembles fine breadcrumbs. Mix in the currants.

Dissolve the yeast in the liquid or, if you are using dried yeast, dissolve the 5ml (1 tsp) caster sugar in the liquid, sprinkle the dried yeast over the top and leave in a warm place until frothy— about 10 minutes. Add the yeast liquid to the dry ingredients all at once and mix to form a firm dough, adding a little extra flour, if needed, until the dough leaves the sides of the bowl clean.

Turn on to a lightly floured surface and knead until smooth, firm and elastic. This should take about 10 minutes by hand or 3–4 minutes if you are using an electric mixer. Shape into a ball and place in a lightly oiled polythene bag with the end secured. Put to rise in a warm place until the dough has doubled in size and springs back when pressed lightly with a floured finger.

Turn out on to a floured surface, knock back and knead for about 2 minutes until smooth. Divide the dough into two equal pieces, and shape to fit 2 greased 450g (1 lb) loaf tins (see p 7 for method of shaping). Place the tins in oiled polythene bags and put to rise in a warm place until the dough reaches the top of the tins. Remove the polythene and bake in a hot oven, 220°C (425°F) mark 7, for 40–45 minutes until the bases of the loaves sound hollow when tapped. Turn on to a wire rack and brush the tops of the loaves immediately with a wet pastry brush dipped in honey or syrup. Leave to cool.

The mixture can also be made into rolls (see p 12 for shaping) but only into round bun shapes. They should be baked in a hot oven, 220°C (425°F) mark 7, for 15–20 minutes. Glaze with honey or syrup as for the loaves.

Variations

Spicy Currant Bread

To the dry ingredients together with the currants add 5ml (1 level tsp) mixed spice, 5ml (1 level tsp) ground cinnamon and the finely grated rind of 1 small lemon. Proceed as for basic currant bread.

Fruited Bread

In place of the 100g (4oz) currants, to the dry ingredients add 100g (4oz) sultanas, raisins or mixed fruit and 50g (2oz) chopped mixed peel. Also, 15–30ml (1–2 tbsp) clear honey can be used to replace the same amount of the liquid. Proceed as for basic currant bread.

Note This bread freezes well.

Malt Bread

A delicious loaf with a sticky top full of sultanas, favoured by many at tea-time.

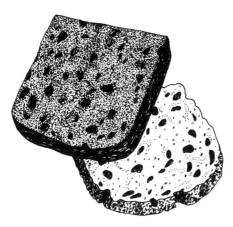

This loaf is made with household flour *not* the strong bread flour.

Ingredients

100g (4oz) malt extract
15ml (1tbsp) black treacle
25g (1oz) margarine
450g (1lb) plain white flour (*not* strong bread flour)
5ml (1 level tsp) salt
175g (6oz) sultanas
25g (1oz) fresh yeast or 15ml (1 level tbsp) dried yeast and 5ml (1 level tsp) caster sugar
Good 150ml ($\frac{1}{4}$pt) warm water, 43°C 110°F
Honey to glaze

Put the malt extract, black treacle and margarine in a saucepan and heat gently until thoroughly blended. Remove from the heat and allow to cool without getting completely cold. Sieve the flour and salt into a large bowl and mix in the sultanas. Dissolve the fresh yeast in the warm water or,

for dried yeast, dissolve 5ml (1tsp) sugar in the water. Sprinkle the dried yeast over the top and leave in a warm place until frothy—about 10 minutes. Add the cooled malt mixture and yeast liquid to the dry ingredients and mix to form a soft and sticky dough. It may be necessary to add a little extra flour in order to make the dough leave the sides of the bowl clean. However, use as little extra flour as possible for this has to be a very soft dough to get the required result.

Turn out on to a lightly floured surface and knead the dough for about 5 minutes until it is smooth and elastic. Divide the dough into two pieces and flatten each piece to an oblong. Roll up like a Swiss roll and shape to fit two greased 450g (1lb) loaf tins, keeping the seam underneath. Place the tins in an oiled polythene bag and put to rise in a warm place until the dough reaches the top of the tins and springs back when lightly pressed with a floured finger. This should take about 1$\frac{1}{2}$ hours in a warm place, but longer in a cool one. Malt bread is a slow riser so don't worry if it takes longer than usual. Remove the polythene and bake in a fairly hot oven, 200°C (400°F) mark 6, for 35–45 minutes, until well risen and brown and the base sounds hollow when tapped. After turning out on to a wire rack, brush the tops of the hot loaves liberally with a wet pastry-brush dipped in honey. Leave to cool.

Note For a darker malt loaf replace 15ml (1tbsp) malt extract with black treacle and, if liked, add a little gravy browning. This loaf will freeze well.

Chelsea Buns

Chelsea buns are, traditionally, rolled up buns with a dried fruit filling. They are cooked to touch each other in a square cake tin and they should be pulled apart when cold to give square-shaped buns. These buns are made by the batter method.

Ingredients

225g (8oz) strong plain white flour
15g ($\frac{1}{2}$oz) fresh yeast or 7.5ml (1$\frac{1}{2}$
    level tsp) dried yeast and 2.5ml ($\frac{1}{2}$
    level tsp) caster sugar
100ml (4fl oz) warm milk, 43°C
    (110°F)
2.5ml ($\frac{1}{2}$ level tsp) salt
15g ($\frac{1}{2}$oz) butter or lard
1 egg, beaten
Approx 50g (approx 2oz) melted butter
    or margarine
100g (4oz) mixed dried fruit
25g (1oz) chopped mixed peel
50g (2oz) soft brown sugar
Clear honey to glaze

Put 50g (2oz) flour into a large bowl, add the fresh yeast or dried yeast, caster sugar and warm milk, and mix to a smooth batter. Put aside in a warm place until the batter froths—this should take 10–20 minutes in a warm place.

Sieve the remaining flour with the salt and rub in the fat. Add this mixture to the yeast batter, together with the beaten egg, and mix to form a soft dough which will leave the sides of the bowl clean after beating the dough. Turn out on to a lightly floured surface and knead the dough until it is smooth and elastic—about 5 minutes. Shape into a ball and place in an oiled polythene bag. Put to rise in a warm place until doubled in size—1–1$\frac{1}{2}$ hours. Grease a 17.5cm (7in) square cake tin. Remove dough from the bag, turn on to a lightly floured surface and knead thoroughly until smooth. Roll out the dough to an oblong about 30cm × 25.5cm (12in × 9in). Brush the whole surface with melted butter or margarine. Mix together the dried fruit and peel and sprinkle evenly over the dough. Sprinkle with brown sugar. Starting from the longest side, roll up the dough like a Swiss roll, sealing the end edge with a little water. Cut the roll into nine even-sized slices and place these evenly, cut-side downwards, in the prepared tin. Cover with oiled polythene and put to rise in a warm place for about 30 minutes or until the dough has risen and feels springy. Remove the polythene and bake in a moderately hot oven, 190 °C (375 °F) mark 5, for 30–35 minutes, until golden brown. Turn all the buns in one piece out on to a wire rack and, whilst still warm, brush the tops with a wet pastry-brush dipped in honey. Leave to get cold. This recipe makes nine buns.

Variations
Chopped glacé cherries, chopped angelica or chopped nuts may be used in place of some of the fruit. Mixed spice or cinnamon may be mixed with the brown sugar, or grated lemon, orange or grapefruit rind added.

Note These buns can be cooked on a greased baking sheet placed well apart. This will give a bun with firm crusty edges all round, unlike the soft pull-apart sides of the traditional Chelsea bun.

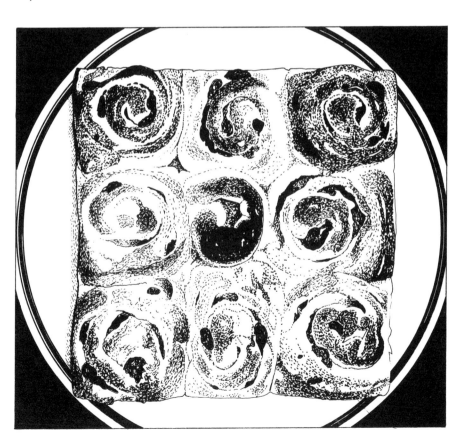

Yorkshire Tea-cakes and Fruity Bannock

Yorkshire Tea-cakes

These large flat tea-cakes can be split open and served with lots of butter. They are at their very best when served slightly warmed and they also toast well.

Ingredients

15g (½oz) fresh yeast or 7.5ml (1½ level tsp) dried yeast and 5ml (1 level tsp) caster sugar
300ml (½pt) warm milk, 43°C (110°F)
450g (1lb) strong plain white flour
5ml (1 level tsp) salt
40g (1½oz) butter or lard
25g (1oz) caster sugar
75g (3oz) currants
25g (1oz) mixed peel (optional)

Blend the fresh yeast in the warm milk. For dried yeast, dissolve 5ml (1tsp) sugar in the milk, then sprinkle the dried yeast over the top and leave in a warm place until frothy—about 10 minutes. Sieve the flour and salt into a bowl, add the butter and rub in until the mixture resembles breadcrumbs. Stir in the sugar, currants and peel until well mixed. Add the yeast liquid to the dry ingredients and mix to form a fairly soft dough, adding a little more flour if necessary to leave the sides of the bowl clean.

Turn out on to a floured surface and knead until smooth and elastic—about 10 minutes by hand or 3–4 minutes if you are using an electric mixer. Shape into a ball and put in a lightly oiled polythene bag. Put to rise in a warm place for about 1 hour or until doubled in size. Turn on to a floured surface, knock back and knead for about 2 minutes until smooth. Divide into five or six equal-sized pieces and knead each into a round, then roll out to a circle 15–17.5cm (6–7in) in diameter. Place the tea-cakes on greased baking sheets and brush the tops with milk. Cover lightly with a sheet of greased polythene and put to rise in a warm place for about 45 minutes or until almost doubled in size. Remove the polythene and bake in a fairly hot oven, 200 °C (400 °F) mark 6, for about 20 minutes. Remove to a wire rack and leave to cool. The tea-cakes can be brushed with honey or syrup, if liked. To serve, split open the tea-cakes and spread thickly with butter, or toast lightly and then spread with butter. This recipe makes five or six large tea-cakes.

Note These tea-cakes can be made smaller, if preferred. Divide the dough into ten or twelve equal-sized pieces and roll out to about 7.5cm (3in). Place on a baking sheet and bake for about 15 minutes.

Fruity Bannock

As a change from the usual scone round, this type of yeasted fruit scone will tempt everyone. It is very easy to make and the fruit and spices can be varied to suit yourself.

Ingredients

225g (8oz) strong plain white flour
25g (1oz) softened butter or margarine
150ml ($\frac{1}{4}$pt) warm milk, 43 °C (110 °F)
15g ($\frac{1}{2}$oz) fresh yeast or 7.5ml (1$\frac{1}{2}$ level tsp) dried yeast and 5ml (1 level tsp) caster sugar
Pinch of salt
25g (1oz) caster sugar
25g (1oz) sultanas
50g (2oz) currants
25g (1oz) chopped mixed peel
Milk to glaze

Put 50g (2oz) flour into a large bowl with the softened butter, warm milk, either fresh yeast or dried yeast and 5ml (1tsp) sugar. Mix well to form a batter and leave in a warm place until frothy—about 20–30 minutes.

Sieve the remaining flour and salt into a bowl and mix in the sugar, sultanas, currants and mixed peel. Add these dry ingredients to the yeast batter and mix well to form a firm dough. Turn on to a lightly floured surface and knead well until smooth, elastic and no longer sticky—about 10 minutes by hand or 3–4 minutes if you are using an electric mixer. Shape into a ball and place in an oiled polythene bag. Put to rise in a warm place until doubled in size. The dough should spring back when pressed gently with a floured finger. This usually takes about 1 hour (see p 5 for alternate rising times). Turn out on to a floured surface, knock back and knead until smooth. Shape into a ball and flatten carefully with your hands to about a 22.5cm (9in) circle, about 1.5cm ($\frac{1}{2}$in) thick. Place on a greased baking sheet and cut into eight wedges with a sharp knife. Brush the top with milk and cover lightly with oiled polythene. Put to rise in a warm place until the dough has doubled in size and feels springy—about 45 minutes. Remove the polythene, brush with milk again, and bake in a fairly hot oven, 200 °C (400 °F) mark 6, for about 20 minutes. Remove to a wire rack and leave to cool. Serve split and buttered, with or without jam, honey, etc.

Note This recipe freezes well, so if you have a freezer it is worth making several of these bannocks in one batch to freeze some for later on.

Bath Buns and SallyLunn

Bath Buns

These are traditionally sweet, uneven and flattish buns with a topping of crushed sugar. The mixture is very soft and is spooned on to the baking sheets. They are often served split and buttered but can also be eaten as they are.

Ingredients

450g (1lb) strong plain white flour
25g (1oz) fresh yeast or 15ml (1 level tbsp) dried yeast
5ml (1 level tsp) caster sugar
60ml (4tbsp) water
150ml ($\frac{1}{4}$pt) milk
5ml (1 level tsp) salt
175g (6oz) sultanas
50g (2oz) chopped mixed peel
50g (2oz) caster sugar
50g (2oz) butter or margarine, melted and cooled but still running
2 eggs, beaten
Little beaten egg
Lightly crushed sugar lumps for topping

Put 100g (4oz) flour into a bowl and add the yeast and 5ml (1tsp) sugar. Warm the water and milk together to about 43°C (110°F), then add to the mixture in the bowl and mix well to form a batter. Set aside in a warm place until frothy—about 10–15 minutes. Sieve together the remaining flour and salt and then mix in the sultanas, mixed peel and sugar. Stir the melted fat and beaten egg into the yeast batter, then add the dry ingredients and mix well to form a soft dough. Turn out on to a floured surface and knead for about 5 minutes until smooth. Place in a lightly floured bowl, cover with oiled polythene and put to rise in a warm place until doubled in size. The length of time required depends on the warmth of the room but it should take 45–60 minutes..

Remove the polythene and beat the mixture with a wooden spoon or your hand to knock out all the air bubbles. Place tablespoonfuls of the mixture well apart on greased baking sheets and cover lightly with oiled polythene. Put to rise in a warm place until the buns double in size. Remove the polythene, brush each bun lightly with beaten egg and sprinkle with lightly crushed sugar lumps. Bake in a moderately hot oven, 190°C (375°F) mark 5, for about 15 minutes, until well risen and golden brown. Cool on a wire rack. This recipe makes about eighteen buns.

Sally Lunn

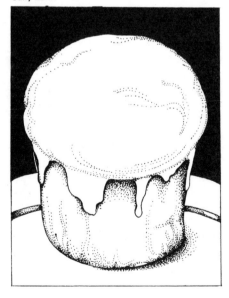

Variations
Sultanas may be replaced by raisins and/or nuts and spices; or finely grated orange or lemon rind may be added to the dry ingredients, but the buns would not then be the true Bath variety.

Sally Lunn

This is a traditional tall, round tea-bread supposed to come from Bath. It is often sliced horizontally and served with butter and jam or honey.

Ingredients

50g (2oz) butter
225ml ($\frac{1}{4}$pt + 4tbsp) milk
5ml (1 level tsp) caster sugar
15g ($\frac{1}{2}$oz) fresh yeast or 10ml (2 level tsp) dried yeast
450g (1lb) strong plain white flour
5ml (1 level tsp) salt
2 eggs, beaten

Sugar Glaze
15ml (1tbsp) water
15ml (1tbsp) sugar

Melt the butter slowly in a pan, then remove from the heat. Stir in the milk and sugar and blend in the fresh or dried yeast. Sieve the flour and salt into a bowl and add the eggs and yeast mixture. Mix to form a soft dough, turn out on to a floured surface and knead well for about 5 minutes until smooth. Divide the dough in half and shape to fit two well greased 12.5cm (5in) round cake tins. Cover loosely with oiled polythene and put to rise in a warm place for about 1 hour, or until the dough fills the tins. Remove the polythene and bake in a very hot oven, 230°C (450°F) mark 8, for 15-20 minutes. Turn out on to a wire rack.

Boil the water and sugar together for 2 minutes, then brush the glaze quickly over the tops of the loaves while they are still warm. Leave to cool.

Pizzas

Pizza is one of the most popular dishes from Italy. It is an open savoury type of tart with a yeasted dough base. It can have a variety of toppings. Tomatoes, onions, herbs, and cheese usually feature and other ingredients such as bacon, salami, sausages, sardines, anchovies, etc give the variety. It can be served either hot or cold. The pizza can be made using left-over white bread dough or brown dough which then is brushed with oil and rolled, as in this recipe. About 450g (1lb) made-up dough is required for a pizza.

Ingredients

15g ($\frac{1}{2}$oz) fresh yeast or 7.5ml (1$\frac{1}{2}$ level tsp) dried yeast
2.5ml ($\frac{1}{2}$ level tsp) caster sugar
Approx 150ml (approx $\frac{1}{4}$pt) warm water, 43°C (110°F)
225g ($\frac{1}{2}$lb) plain white flour (preferably strong)
5ml (1 level tsp) salt
15g ($\frac{1}{2}$oz) lard or margarine
Oil

Topping

450g (1lb) onions, peeled and thinly sliced
822g (1lb 13oz) canned tomatoes or 450g (1lb) fresh tomatoes, skinned and sliced
10ml (2 level tsp) oregano or basil
Salt and pepper
175g (6oz) Bel Paese or processed cheese, sliced
1 can anchovies, drained
Black or stuffed green olives

Blend the fresh yeast and sugar in the warm water. For dried yeast, dissolve the sugar in the water, then sprinkle the dried yeast over the top and put in a warm place until frothy—about 10 minutes. Sieve the flour and salt into a bowl and rub in the fat. Add the yeast liquid to the dry ingredients and mix to form a fairly firm dough. Turn out on to a lightly floured surface and knead until smooth and elastic—about 10 minutes by hand or 3–4 minutes if you are using an electric mixer. Shape into a ball, place in a lightly oiled polythene bag, secure the end, and put to rise in a warm place until doubled in size. This should take $\frac{3}{4}$–1 hour in a warm place or about 2 hours at room temperature.

Turn the dough out on to a lightly floured surface, knock back and roll out to a long narrow strip. Brush all over with oil, then roll up like a Swiss roll. Carefully roll out again to a long strip and brush again with oil and roll up. Repeat this process twice more. To make one large pizza, grease a 30cm (12in) plain flan ring and place on a greased baking sheet. For two smaller pizzas, use two 20cm (8in) rings (the pizzas can be made without a ring, but some of the topping will probably slide off). Roll out the dough to one 30cm (12in) circle or two 20cm (8in) circles. Place on the greased baking sheets inside the rings and brush all over the dough with oil.

For the topping, sauté the onions in 15–30ml (1–2 tbsp) oil until soft and just beginning to colour. Spoon over the dough leaving a 2cm ($\frac{3}{4}$in) margin all round. If using canned tomatoes, partly drain and then lay them over the onions, or arrange the skinned, sliced fresh tomatoes evenly over the onions.

Sprinkle with herbs and then season well. Put to rise for 15 minutes in a warm place. Bake in a very hot oven 230°C (450°F) mark 8, for 20 minutes. Remove from the oven and quickly cover the pizza with the sliced cheese and arrange a lattice or cartwheel pattern with the anchovies. Decorate with black or stuffed olives and return to the oven for a further 20 minutes. Cover lightly with foil if getting too brown (smaller pizzas will take a little less time). Remove the rings and serve hot or leave to cool and serve cold with salads. This recipe serves four to six portions.

Bacon and Mushroom Pizza

Topping

25g (1oz) butter
1 clove garlic, crushed (optional)
100–175g (4–6oz) mushrooms, sliced
830g (1lb 13oz) can skinned
  tomatoes or 450g (1lb) fresh
  tomatoes, skinned and sliced
10ml (2 level tsp) mixed herbs
Salt and pepper
100g (4oz) Cheddar cheese, coarsely
  grated
225g ($\frac{1}{2}$lb) streaky bacon rashers,
  derinded
Few pickled walnuts or stuffed green
  olives

Melt the butter in a pan and fry the garlic and mushrooms until soft. Arrange over the prepared pizza dough base. Cover with sliced tomatoes or partly drained canned tomatoes, then sprinkle first with herbs and then with salt and pepper. Sprinkle the cheese over the herbs and arrange the bacon rashers in a lattice or cartwheel pattern. Fill in the gaps with pieces of pickled walnut or olives. Put to rise in a warm place for 15 minutes. Bake in a very hot oven, 230°C (450°F) mark 8, for 30–40 minutes (smaller pizzas will take a little less time).

43

Doughnuts

Large, sticky, sugar-covered buns with a jam filling, doughnuts are deep-fried until golden brown and then coated in caster sugar or a cinnamon and sugar mixture. They can also be fried without a filling, and when cold, be split open and filled with whipped cream and/or jam. Round American-style doughnuts are made using two pastry cutters to make the circles and are then fried in the same way.

Ingredients

225g (8oz) strong plain white flour
2.5ml ($\frac{1}{2}$ level tsp) salt
15g ($\frac{1}{2}$oz) fresh yeast or 10ml (2 level tsp) dried yeast and 2.5ml (1 level tsp) caster sugar
Approx 60ml (4 tbsp) warm milk, 43°C (110°F)
15g ($\frac{1}{2}$oz) softened butter or margarine
1 egg, beaten
Deep fat or oil for frying
Caster sugar and ground cinnamon for coating

Sieve the flour and salt into a bowl. Blend the fresh yeast in the warm milk or, for dried yeast, dissolve 5ml (1 tsp) sugar in the milk, then sprinkle the dried yeast over the top and leave in a warm place until frothy—about 10 minutes. Add the yeast liquid to the dry ingredients with the softened butter and beaten egg and mix to form a fairly soft dough which leaves the sides of the bowl clean, adding a little more milk, if necessary.

Turn out on to a floured surface and knead thoroughly until smooth—about 10 minutes by hand or 3–4 minutes if you are using an electric mixer. Place the dough in a lightly floured bowl, cover with oiled polythene and put to rise until doubled in size. This should take 45–60 minutes in a warm place; 2 hours at room temperature; up to 12 hours in a cold larder, or up to 24 hours in a refrigerator. Remember to allow refrigerated dough to return to room temperature before proceeding.

Turn out again on to a floured surface and knock back and knead for about 2 minutes until smooth. Divide into eight pieces and roll each piece into a round. Put 5ml (1 level tsp) stiff raspberry jam in the centre and draw up the edges to form a ball, making sure the dough is well joined together to enclose the jam. Put the buns on to greased and floured baking sheets, cover with oiled polythene and put to rise for 10–15 minutes until a little puffy. Heat a pan of fat or oil to 182°C (360°F) or until a 2.5cm (1in) cube of bread will brown in 1 minute.

Fry the doughnuts, a few at a time, for 5–10 minutes until golden brown. Drain thoroughly on crumpled kitchen paper and, whilst still hot, coat either in plain caster sugar or a mixture of caster sugar mixed with ground cinnamon to taste. The easist way to do this is to put the coating in a polythene bag, add the doughnuts one at a time and shake until well coated. Remove and leave to cool. Reheat the fat and cook the remaining doughnuts in the same way.

Cream Doughnuts

Shape the pieces of dough either into balls or oval shapes and put to rise as before. Fry in hot fat for 5–10 minutes until golden brown and drain and coat in sugar as before. When cold, make a

slit along the top of each doughnut and either fill with slightly sweetened whipped cream, or first add a little jam of your choice and then cover with the whipped cream.

Ring Doughnuts

Roll out the whole piece of dough to about 1 cm ($\frac{1}{2}$in) thickness. Using a 7.5cm (3in) plain round cutter, cut into rounds. Then cut out the centres of each doughnut using a smaller cutter, 2.5–4cm (1–1$\frac{1}{2}$in). Transfer the rings to a greased and floured baking sheet, cover with oiled polythene and put to rise until almost doubled in size. Use the remaining dough trimmings to make more doughnuts. Fry the doughnuts a few at a time in hot deep fat until golden brown—about 5 minutes. Drain on absorbent kitchen paper and coat in sugar as for jam doughnuts. Leave to cool. These doughnuts are usually eaten as they are, but can also have either a little whipped cream piped around the top of each one, or be split open and filled with jam and/or cream.

Note Doughnuts must be eaten whilst fresh. The jam can be put into the doughnuts after proving the buns just prior to baking. To do this, make a small hole in the side and fill with jam using a long piping nozzle fitted into a bag. Make sure the hole is completely closed before cooking.

Iced Plait

An attractive, rich yeasted bread in the shape of a plait which can either be served decorated with nuts and glacé cherries or with glacé icing and the nuts and cherries.

Ingredients

225g (8oz) strong plain white flour
Pinch of salt
25g (1oz) butter or margarine
50g (2oz) caster sugar
75g (3oz) mixed dried fruit
15g ($\frac{1}{2}$oz) fresh yeast or 7.5ml (1$\frac{1}{2}$ level tsp) dried yeast and 5ml (1 level tsp) caster sugar

75ml (5 tbsp) warm milk, 43 °C (110 °F)
1 egg, beaten
Beaten egg to glaze
Chopped nuts and glacé cherries for decoration

Sieve the flour and salt into a bowl and rub in the butter or margarine. Mix in the sugar and dried fruit. Dissolve the fresh yeast in the milk. For dried yeast, dissolve 5ml (1tsp) sugar in the milk, sprinkle the dried yeast over the top and leave in a warm place until frothy—about 10 minutes. Add the yeast liquid to the dry ingredients together with the egg and mix to form a fairly soft dough.

Turn out on to a lightly floured surface and knead until smooth and elastic—about 10 minutes by hand or 3–4 minutes if you are using an electric mixer. Shape into a ball and place in an oiled polythene bag. Put to rise in a warm place for about 1 hour until doubled in size and the dough springs back when lightly pressed with a floured finger (see p 5 for alternate rising times).

Turn out on to a floured surface, knock back and knead for about 2 minutes until smooth and firm. Divide into three equal pieces and roll each piece to a long, thin sausage. Place these pieces side-by-side and, beginning in the middle, plait the three pieces together towards you ; secure the ends. Turn the dough right over and plait the remaining pieces to complete the loaf, securing the end. Place on a greased baking sheet. Cover with a sheet of oiled polythene and put to rise in a warm place for about 25 minutes or until doubled in size. Remove the polythene, brush all over with beaten

Glacé Icing

225g (8oz) icing sugar
20–30ml (1½–2 tbsp) warm water, or
orange or lemon juice
Colouring (optional)

Blend the sieved icing sugar and water or fruit juice in a basin until smooth, adding colouring sparingly, if liked. This mixture gives a soft, flowing icing ; for a firmer consistency, use only 10–15ml (¾–1tbsp) water.

egg and bake in a hot oven, 220°C (425°F) mark 7, for about 15 minutes, until golden brown. Cool on a wire rack. Either brush with a wet brush dipped in honey and sprinkle thickly with chopped nuts and pieces of glacé cherry, or leave until cold and then coat with glacé icing (see below) and sprinkle with the nuts and cherries. Leave to set.

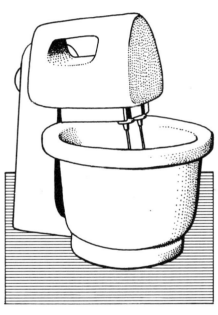

Variations
The plait can also be shaped into a crescent after plaiting or have the two ends of the plait joined together to make a circle. Place on greased baking sheets and put to rise and bake as above.

Iced Fruit Buns

Divide the dough into 50g (2oz) pieces and either shape into buns by rolling each piece on a lightly floured surface with the palm of your hand or divide each piece into two and roll to thin sausage shapes and then twist together securing each end. Place on greased baking sheets, cover with oiled polythene and put to rise until doubled in size. Bake for 10–15 minutes. Decorate as for the plait.

Devonshire Splits

These buns are popular for they are served split and filled with Devonshire or clotted cream and jam. They are often enjoyed on holidays in the West Country as part of a cream tea.

Ingredients

15g (½oz) fresh yeast or 7.5ml (1½ level tsp) dried yeast and 5ml (1 level tsp) caster sugar
Approx 300ml (½pt) warm milk, 43°C (110°F)
450g (1lb) strong plain white flour ·
5ml (1 level tsp) salt
50g (2oz) butter or margarine
25g (1oz) caster sugar
Devonshire or whipped cream
Raspberry jam
Icing sugar

Blend the fresh yeast in half the warm milk. For dried yeast, dissolve 5ml (1tsp) sugar in the milk, then sprinkle the dried yeast over the top and leave in a warm place until frothy—about 10 minutes. Sieve the flour and salt into a bowl. Dissolve the butter or margarine and the sugar in the remaining milk, then cool to 43°C (110°F) before adding to the dry ingredients together with the yeast liquid. Beat to form a soft, elastic dough, then turn on to a floured surface and knead until smooth —about 10 minutes by hand or 3–4 minutes if you are using an electric mixer.

Shape into a ball, put into an oiled polythene bag and put to rise until doubled in size—about 1 hour in a warm place; 2 hours at room temperature; up to 12 hours in a cold larder or up to 24 hours in a refrigerator. Remember to allow the

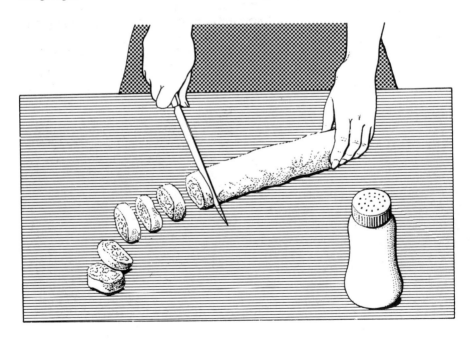

dough to return to room temperature before shaping—about 1 hour.

Turn the dough on to a floured surface, and divide into fifteen even-sized pieces. Knead each piece lightly and shape into a ball. Place on greased baking sheets and slightly flatten each bun with the palm of your hand. Cover with sheets of oiled polythene and put to rise in a warm place for about 25 minutes or until doubled in size. Bake in a hot oven, 220°C (425°F) mark 7, for 15–20 minutes. Remove to a wire rack and leave to cool. Before serving, split the buns open and spread with jam and cream. Reassemble the buns and dredge the top of each one with icing sugar. This recipe makes fifteen buns.

Note These buns freeze well but do not fill until properly thawed and ready to serve. Stale buns can be toasted first.

Swiss Buns

Divide the knocked-back dough into 50–75g (2–3oz) pieces and then shape each piece into a sausage shape using the palms of your hands. Place on well greased baking sheets. Cover with a sheet of oiled polythene and put to rise in a warm place until doubled in size. Remove polythene and bake in a hot oven, 220°C (425°F) mark 7, for about 15 minutes, until well risen and pale golden brown. Remove to a wire rack and leave to cool.

Make up a glacé icing by sieving 225g (8oz) icing sugar into a bowl and adding sufficient warm water and a little cochineal (if liked) to give a thick coating consistency. Spoon over the buns and leave to set.

Hot Cross Buns

The traditional spicy fruit bun for Easter. It is suitable to eat at any meal but often favoured for breakfast served warm with lots of butter or at tea-time either warmed or toasted. The crosses can be made in several ways. The easiest and quickest way is simply to cut a cross into the top of the bun after shaping, and then mark it again after proving, immediately before putting into the oven. Narrow strips of pastry are definitely more visible but do require the extra time to make a small amount of short crust pastry. Both methods are given here.

Ingredients

450g (1 lb) strong plain white flour
25g (1 oz) fresh yeast or 15ml (1 level tbsp) dried yeast
5ml (1 level tsp) caster sugar
150ml ($\frac{1}{4}$ pt) warm milk, 43°C (110°F)
60ml (4 tbsp) warm water, 43°C (110°F)
5ml (1 level tsp) salt
2.5ml ($\frac{1}{2}$ level tsp) ground nutmeg
2.5ml ($\frac{1}{2}$ level tsp) mixed spice
2.5ml ($\frac{1}{2}$ level tsp) ground cinnamon
50g (2oz) caster sugar
50g (2oz) chopped mixed peel
100g (4oz) currants
50g (2oz) melted butter or margarine, cooled
1 egg beaten

Pastry for Crosses (optional)

60g (2oz) plain four
Pinch of salt
15g ($\frac{1}{2}$oz) margarine
15g ($\frac{1}{2}$oz) lard or white fat
Water to mix

Sugar Glaze
45ml (3 level tbsp) caster sugar
45–60ml (3–4 tbsp) milk and water mixed

Place 100g (4oz) flour in a large bowl with fresh or dried yeast and 5ml (1 tsp) sugar. Add the warm milk and water and mix well. Put in a warm place until the batter becomes frothy—this should take 10–15 minutes for fresh yeast or 20–25 minutes for dried yeast.

Sieve the remaining flour into a bowl with the salt and spices, and then mix in the sugar followed by the mixed peel and currants. Add the cooled melted butter and beaten egg to the yeast batter, followed by all the dry ingredients, and mix together to form a softish dough. Turn out on to a lightly floured surface and knead until smooth and no longer sticky—about 10 minutes by hand or 3–4 minutes if you are using an electric mixer. Shape into a ball and place in a lightly oiled polythene bag. Put to rise in a warm place for about 1$\frac{1}{2}$–2 hours until doubled in size and the dough springs

back when lightly pressed with a floured finger. This is a richly fruited dough, so it takes longer to rise than ordinary plain bread.

Turn out again on to a lightly floured surface. Knock back and knead for about 2 minutes until smooth. Divide the dough into twelve or fourteen even-sized pieces. Shape each piece into a bun by rolling on a hard surface with the palm of your hand, first of all pressing down hard, and then easing the pressure as the bun takes shape. Place the buns fairly well apart on a lightly greased baking sheet. Either cut a cross into each bun using a very sharp knife or, if using pastry crosses, leave as they are. Cover with a sheet of oiled polythene and put to rise in a warm place until doubled in size— about 30 minutes. For simple crosses, mark again using a very sharp knife and bake in a moderately hot oven, 190°C (375°F) mark 5, for 20–25 minutes until golden brown. For pastry cross buns, while the buns are rising, make up the shortcrust pastry by rubbing the fats into the flour with a pinch of salt added, until the mixture resembles fine breadcrumbs, then mix to a pliable dough with a little cold water. Roll out very thinly on a floured surface and cut into very narrow strips about 8.5cm ($3\frac{1}{2}$in) long. Brush the strips with milk and lay two across each bun to make a cross. Bake in a moderately hot oven as for the other buns.

While the buns are cooking, make the sugar glaze by mixing the sugar, milk and water together in a small pan and bring to the boil for 2 minutes. Leave to cool. Remove the buns to a wire rack and, while still hot, brush the tops two or three times with the sugar glaze and then leave to cool.

Note These buns freeze well.

Lardy Cake and Dough Cake

Both these cakes are made from basic white bread dough with the extra ingredients added after the first rising. When baking a batch of white bread, remove a little of the dough and use to make a different sort of cake for the family. Lardy cake can be served at tea-time or warmed and served as a pudding with cream or custard.

Lardy Cake

Ingredients

675g (1½lb) risen white bread dough, using 450g (1lb) flour (see p 6)
100g (4oz) lard or half lard and half margarine
100g (4oz) caster sugar
5ml (1 level tsp) mixed spice or cinnamon
75–100g (3–4oz) sultanas, or currants, or mixed dried druit

Remove the dough from the polythene bag and knock back. Knead well until smooth. Roll out on a floured surface to 5mm (¼in) thickness. Cover the dough with small flakes made from 50g (2oz) fat and then sprinkle with 50g (2oz) sugar, followed by 2.5ml (½tsp) spice and 40–50g (1½–2oz) dried fruit. Roll up loosely like a Swiss roll and then roll out again to an oblong. Repeat, covering the dough with the remaining fat, most of the sugar, and all the spice and fruit. Roll up loosely again. Roll out to an oblong and roll up for a third time and place in a greased baking tin about 25cm × 20cm (10in × 8in) pressing the dough down firmly to fit into the corners. Cover with a sheet of oiled polythene and put to rise in a warm place until doubled in size. Remove polythene, brush the top of the cake with oil and sprinkle with the remaining sugar. Using a sharp knife, score the top into a criss-cross pattern. Bake in a hot oven, 220°C 425°F) mark 7, for about 30 minutes. Turn out and cool on a wire rack and serve in slices either plain or buttered.

Dough Cake

A tea-bread which can be varied by adding orange or lemon rind, other spices or a tablespoon of black treacle.

Making lardy cake

Spread fruit and spices over dough

Roll up loosely

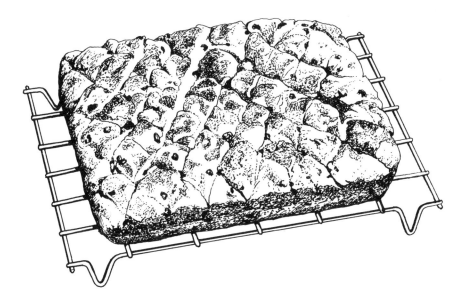

Lardy cake

Ingredients

450g (1 lb) risen white bread dough
(see p 6)
50g (2oz) butter or margarine,
softened
50g (2oz) caster sugar
100g (4oz) mixed dried druit
50g (2oz) chopped nuts
5ml (1 level tsp) mixed spice
Honey or syrup to glaze

Remove the dough from the polythene
bag and place in a bowl. Add all the
other ingredients, and knead and
squeeze the mixture until evenly
blended. Shape the dough to fit a
greased 450g (1 lb) loaf tin and put into
a large oiled polythene bag. Put to rise
in a warm place until the dough reaches
the top of the tin. Remove the
polythene and bake in a very hot oven,
230°C (450°F) mark 8, for about 30

minutes, until the base sounds hollow
when tapped. Remove from the tin to a
wire rack and brush the top of the hot
loaf with a wet pastry-brush dipped in
honey or syrup to glaze. Leave to cool.

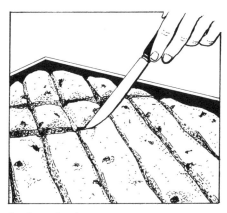

Scoring lardy cake

53

Scandinavian Tea Ring

A most attractive but simple to make tea-ring with a spicy sugar filling which will delight your guests. A variety of toppings can be added either on top of glacé icing or straight on to the ring after brushing with honey or syrup.

Ingredients

225g (8oz) strong plain white flour
2.5ml ($\frac{1}{2}$ level tsp) caster sugar
15g ($\frac{1}{2}$oz) fresh yeast or 7.5ml
   (1$\frac{1}{2}$ level tsp) dried yeast
100ml (4fl oz) warm milk, 43°C
   (110°F)
2.5ml ($\frac{1}{2}$ level tsp) salt
25g (1oz) margarine
$\frac{1}{2}$ egg, beaten
20g ($\frac{3}{4}$oz) melted butter or margarine
50–75g (2–3oz) soft brown sugar
10–15ml (2–3 level tsp) ground
   cinnamon or mixed spice
Glacé cherries, chopped angelica
   and/or flaked almonds or chopped
   walnuts for topping

Lemon Glacé Icing

100g (4oz) icing sugar, sieved
5ml ($\frac{1}{2}$ level tsp) finely grated
   lemon rind
Lemon juice

Put 65g (2$\frac{1}{2}$oz) flour with the sugar, fresh or dried yeast and milk into a bowl. Put aside in a warm place for about 20 minutes until frothy and the yeast dissolved. Sieve the remaining flour with the salt into a bowl and rub in the margarine until the mixture resembles fine breadcrumbs. Add the beaten egg and the flour mixture to the yeast batter and mix well to give a fairly soft dough which will leave the sides of the bowl clean.

Turn the dough on to a lightly floured surface and knead until it is smooth and no longer sticky—about 10 minutes by hand or 3–4 minutes if you are using an electric mixer (no extra flour should be necessary). Form the dough into a ball and place in a lightly oiled polythene bag, tie loosely and put to rise in a warm place until doubled in size—about 1 hour (see p 5 for alternate rising times).

Remove the risen dough from the polythene bag on to a lightly floured surface. Knock back and knead for about 2 minutes until smooth. Roll out the dough to an oblong on a floured surface to approx 30cm × 22.5cm (12in × 9in). Brush all over with the melted butter or margarine and then sprinkle with a mixture of brown sugar and spice. Starting from the long edge, roll up the dough tightly like a Swiss roll, sealing the ends together to form a ring. Place on a well greased baking sheet. Using scissors which have been brushed with oil, cut slashes at an

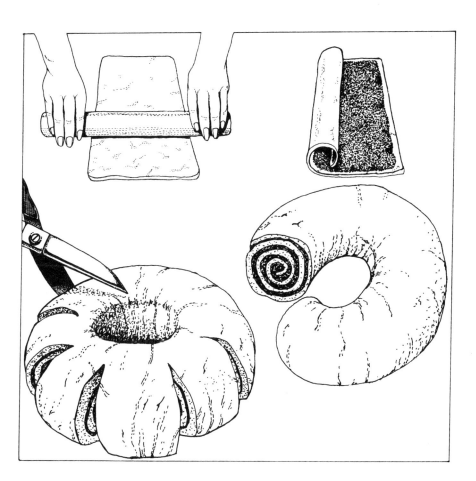

angle into the ring about two-thirds of the way through the dough at 2.5cm (1in) intervals. Keeping a neat shape, carefully turn the cut sections to one side to open up the ring a little.

Cover with oiled polythene and put to rise in a warm place for about 30 minutes until well risen. Remove the polythene and bake in a moderately hot oven, 190°C (375°F) mark 5, for 30–35 minutes, until well risen and golden brown. Remove the ring carefully to a wire rack.

While the ring is still warm, make the glacé icing by mixing the icing sugar and lemon rind with sufficient lemon juice to give a thick coating consistency. Spoon over the tea-ring, allowing the icing to drip down over the cut pieces. Decorate the top with cherries, angelica and nuts, as you wish. Leave to cool and set before cutting.

Danish Pastries

To achieve the required soft dough for these delicious pastries, use household plain flour—not the strong bread flour. This softer flour, together with the softened butter and folding and rolling involved, gives a very tender, flaky pastry. The fillings and toppings can be varied according to taste, and your own special fillings can be added to give a wider choice. These pastries are a Danish speciality but are easy and fairly quick to make.

Ingredients

25g (1oz) fresh yeast or 15ml (1 level tbsp) dried yeast and 5ml (1 level tsp) caster sugar
Approx 150ml (approx ¼pt) water
450g (1lb) plain, not strong, flour
5ml (1 level tsp) salt
50g (2oz) lard
25g (1oz) caster sugar
2 eggs, beaten
300g (10oz) butter
Beaten egg to glaze

Blend the fresh yeast with the water. For dried yeast, dissolve the sugar in warm water 43°C (110°F), then sprinkle the dried yeast over the top and leave in a warm place until frothy—about 10 minutes.

Sieve the flour and salt into a bowl, rub in the lard; then mix in the sugar. Add the yeast liquid and beaten eggs to the dry ingredients and mix to form a soft, elastic dough, adding a little more water if necessary. Turn out on to a lightly floured surface and knead lightly by hand for about 2–3 minutes, until smooth. Put the dough into a

lightly oiled polythene bag and chill in a refrigerator for 10 minutes. Soften the butter with a knife and shape into an oblong about 10cm × 25cm (4in × 10in). Roll out the dough on a lightly floured surface to a 27.5cm (11in) square and spread the rectangle of butter down the centre third of the dough. Enclose the butter by folding the two flaps of pastry over to just overlap in the middle, and seal the top and bottom with the rolling-pin.

Turn the dough so that the folds are to the sides and roll into a strip three times as long as it is wide. Fold the bottom third of the dough upwards and the top third down and seal the edges. Put in the polythene bag and put to rest in a refrigerator for 10 minutes. Repeat the rolling, folding and resting of the dough twice more, leaving it to chill for 30 minutes after the last folding. The dough is then ready for use.

Make up the required fillings and prepare the toppings.

Fillings

Almond Paste

15g (½oz) butter
75g (3oz) caster sugar
75g (3oz) ground almonds
1 egg, beaten
Almond essence

Cream the butter and sugar together until soft, then stir in the almonds and add sufficient egg to mix to a pliable consistency. Add a few drops of almond essence to taste.

Cinnamon Butter

50g (2oz) butter
50g (2oz) caster sugar
10ml (2 level tsp) ground cinnamon

Cream the butter and sugar together until fluffy and then beat in the ground cinnamon until well mixed.

Confectioner's Custard

1 whole egg, separated
1 egg yolk
50g (2oz) caster sugar
30ml (2 level tbsp) plain flour
30ml (2 level tbsp) cornflour
300ml (½pt) milk
Vanilla essence

Cream the egg yolks and sugar together in a bowl until really thick and pale in colour. Beat in the flour and cornflour and a little cold milk to

make a smooth paste. Heat the rest of the milk gently (preferably in a non-stick pan) until almost boiling and, stirring continuously, pour on to the egg mixture. Return the mixture to the saucepan and, continuing to stir, cook slowly over a gentle heat, until the mixture just comes to the boil. Remove the saucepan from the heat. Whisk the egg whites until stiff and fold into the custard. Add vanilla essence to taste and return the pan to cook over a very gentle heat for 2–3 minutes. Cool before using. Cover the pan with a lid or cling-film, to prevent a skin forming whilst cooling.

Dried Fruit Filling

25g (1oz) butter
25g (1oz) brown sugar
Pinch of ground nutmeg
25g (1oz) currants
25g (1oz) sultanas

Cream the butter and sugar together. Beat in nutmeg to taste and the dried fruits.

Toppings
Apricot jam or redcurrant jelly
Flaked and chopped almonds, plain and toasted
Glacé cherries and angelica

White Glacé Icing

100–175g (4–6oz) icing sugar, sieved
Little flavouring essence (optional)
15–30ml (1–2 tbsp) warm water

Put the icing sugar into a bowl and add flavouring essence. Gradually beat in sufficient warm water to give a thick coating consistency. Add more water or sugar to adjust the consistency.

Shaping and Baking Danish Pastries

Crescents

Roll out thinly one quarter of the dough into a 22.5cm (9in) circle. Cut this circle into eight even-sized wedges. Put 1 tsp almond paste, confectioner's custard, dried fruit filling (see p 57) or even a little stewed apple at the wide base of each piece of dough. Roll carefully and fairly loosely to the point. Curve into a crescent shape and place on a lightly greased baking sheet. Cover lightly with oiled polythene and put to rise in a warm place for 20–30 minutes until puffy. Brush with beaten egg and bake in a hot oven, 220 °C (425 °F) mark 7, for 10–15 minutes. Remove to a wire rack and, while still hot, brush with a little white glacé icing (see p 57) and sprinkle with nuts. Leave until cold and set. This recipe makes eight pastries.

Windmills and Imperial Stars

Roll out thinly one quarter of the dough and cut into 7.5cm (3in) squares. Make diagonal cuts from each corner to within 1cm ($\frac{1}{2}$in) of the centre. Put a piece of almond paste in the middle and fold one corner of each cut section to the centre of the square securing each tip with a little beaten egg. Place on a greased baking sheet. Cover with lightly oiled polythene and put to rise in a warm place for 20–30 minutes until puffy, then brush with beaten egg and bake in a hot oven, 220 °C (425 °F) mark 7, for about 20 minutes. Remove to a wire rack and, while still hot, brush with white glacé icing (see p 57) and sprinkle with toasted flaked almonds

and pieces of glacé cherry and/or angelica to make windmills. For imperial stars, finish the centres with a spoonful of confectioner's custard (see p 57) and possibly a piece of glacé cherry, and brush the star projections with glacé icing. Leave to cool and set.

Fruit Pinwheels

Roll out thinly one quarter of the dough and cut into an oblong 30cm × 20cm (12in × 8in). Spread all over with the dried fruit filling (see p 57), adding a little chopped mixed peel and chopped glacé cherries, if liked. Roll up like a Swiss roll from the short end, securing the end with beaten egg. Cut into 2.5cm (1in) thick slices and place, cut-side downward, on a greased baking sheet. Flatten slightly. Cover with oiled polythene and put to rise in a warm place until puffy—about 20 minutes. Brush with beaten egg and bake in a hot oven, 220 °C (425 °F) mark 7, for 15–20 minutes, until golden brown. Remove to a wire rack and either brush with glacé icing or with a

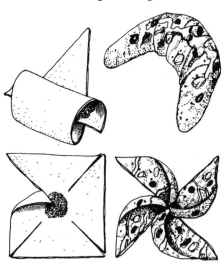

wet pastry-brush dipped in honey and sprinkle with toasted flaked almonds. Leave to cool and set. This recipe makes eight pastries.

Cocks Combs

Roll out one quarter of the dough and cut into strips 11cm × 12.5cm (4½in × 5in). Spread half the width of each strip with almond paste, confectioner's custard (see p 57) or stewed apple sprinkled with cinnamon and currants. Fold over the other half, sealing the edges with beaten egg. Make four or five cuts into the folded edge of the pastry and place on a greased baking sheet, curving it to open out the comb. Cover with oiled polythene, put to rise in a warm place until puffy—about 20 minutes. Brush with beaten egg and bake in a hot oven, 220°C (425°F) mark 7, for about 20 minutes. Remove to a wire rack and, while still hot, brush with glacé icing and sprinkle with toasted almonds. This recipe makes six to eight pastries.

Cushions

Roll out thinly one quarter of the dough and cut into 7.5cm (3in) squares. Put a little almond paste, confectioner's custard or other filling to taste (see p 57) in the centre and either fold two alternate corners to overlap slightly in the centre and secure with beaten egg, or fold all four corners into the centre to overlap a little and secure with beaten egg. Place on greased baking sheets and cover with oiled polythene. Put to rise in a warm place for 20–30 minutes until puffy, then brush with beaten egg and bake in a hot oven, 220°C (425°F) mark 7, for about 15 minutes. Remove to a wire rack and, while still hot, brush lightly with glacé icing (see p 57). Sprinkle with nuts and cherries and put a spoonful of confectioner's custard (see p 57) or redcurrant jelly in the centre of each one. This recipe makes eight pastries.

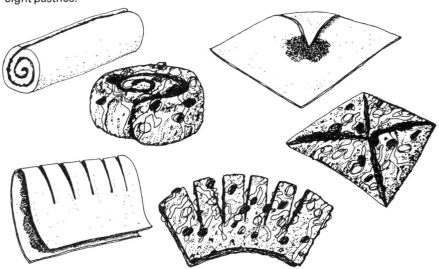

Croissants

These are the classic crisp and flaky rolls of a continental breakfast, the taste of which often lingers long after a holiday. They are best served warm. The secret of making a good croissant is to have both the dough and the fat firm so that they make two definite layers. The pastry is light because it is made by a combination of two methods of aeration : the yeast fermentation of a rich yeast dough, and the trapping of air with the fat as in flaky pastry. The pastry must be kept cold throughout the preparation with only the final rising at a warm temperature after shaping. To get the layering even, roll the dough thinly and use a margarine that is hard and waxy—not a soft type at room temperature. The dough must be wrapped in polythene each time when chilled to prevent cracking and a skin forming. Whilst rolling, keep the dough in shape with straight sides and square corners to make the folding up and layering even, and work quickly when handling the dough to prevent it from becoming soft and warm.

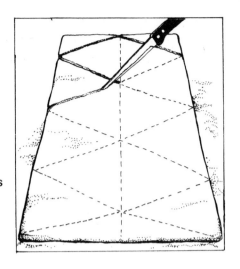

Ingredients

25g (1oz) fresh yeast or 15ml (1 level tbsp) dried yeast and 5ml (1 level tsp) caster sugar
300ml less 60ml (½pt less 4tbsp) warm water 43°C (110°F)
450g (1lb) strong plain white flour
10ml (2 level tsp) salt
25g (1oz) lard
1 egg, beaten
100–175g (4–6oz) hard margarine

Egg Glaze

1 egg, beaten
2.5ml (½ level tsp) caster sugar
15–30ml (1–2 tbsp) water

Blend the fresh yeast into the water. For dried yeast, dissolve the sugar in the water, then sprinkle the dried yeast over the top and leave in a warm place until frothy—about 10 minutes. Sieve the flour and salt together into a bowl, add the lard and rub in. Add the yeast liquid and beaten egg, and mix well to form a dough. Turn out on to a lightly floured surface and knead thoroughly until smooth and even—10–15 minutes by hand or about 5 minutes if you are using an electric mixer.

Roll out the dough to a rectangle about 50cm × 20cm × 5mm (20in × 8in × ¼in) thick, taking care to keep the edges straight and the corners square. Divide the margarine into three. Soften each piece of margarine with a knife, then use one part to dot evenly over the top two-thirds of the dough, leaving a small

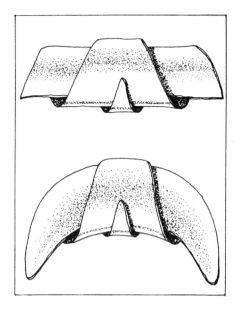

border clear all round. Fold into three by bringing up the bottom plain third first, then folding the top third over the other two. Turn the dough so that the fold is on the right-hand side and then seal the edges with a rolling-pin. Roll out the dough gently again to a long strip by gently pressing the dough at intervals with the rolling-pin. Repeat with the other two portions of margarine, taking care all the time to keep the dough in a neat rectangle. Place the dough in a lightly oiled polythene bag and put to rest in a refrigerator for 30 minutes.

Remove from the bag and roll out and fold as before (without adding any fat, of course) three times more. Replace in the polythene bag and return to the refrigerator for at least 1 hour. The dough can be left in the refrigerator overnight or for two or three days at this stage, ready to make into croissants at any time.

Shaping Croissants

Roll the dough out on a lightly floured surface to a rectange about 57.5cm × 35cm (23in × 14in). Cover with lightly oiled polythene and leave to rest for 10 minutes. Trim the dough to 52.5cm × 30cm (21in × 12in) and then cut in half lengthwise. Cut each strip into six triangles 15cm (6in) high with a 15cm (6in) base (see diagram). Make the egg glaze by mixing together the egg, sugar and water and use to brush all over the dough. Roll up each triangle loosely, starting from the wide base to the point and finishing with the tip underneath. Bend into a crescent shape and place on ungreased baking sheets. Brush the top of each croissant with egg glaze and put each baking sheet into a lightly oiled polythene bag. Close bags and put to rise at room temperature for about 30 minutes, until light and puffy. Remove the polythene and brush again with egg glaze. Bake in a hot oven, 220°C (425°F) mark 7, for about 20 minutes. This recipe makes twelve croissants.

Note Croissants are best served warm. To reheat, wrap lightly in foil before putting into a hot oven for a few minutes.

Soda Bread and Scone Rounds

Soda Bread (*without yeast*)

Ingredients

450g (1lb) plain white flour
10ml (2 level tsp) bicarbonate of soda
10ml (2 level tsp) cream of tartar
5ml (1 level tsp) salt
50g (2oz) lard or margarine
15ml (1 tbsp) lemon juice
300ml (½pt) milk

Sieve together into a bowl the flour, bicarbonate of soda, cream of tartar and salt. Rub in the lard or margarine until the mixture resembles fine breadcrumbs. Add the lemon juice to the milk to make it turn sour (or use sour milk or buttermilk, if available), and add this to the dry ingredients and mix to a soft manageable dough, using a palette knife. Turn on to a floured surface and, using your hands, shape into a round about 17.5cm (7in) across.

Transfer the dough to a greased baking sheet and mark into quarters with a sharp knife. Dredge the top with flour or sprinkle with coarse sea salt.

Bake in a hot oven, 220°C (425°F) mark 7, for about 30 minutes, until well risen and golden brown. Cool on a wire rack and eat whilst fresh—stale soda bread is very unpalatable.

Brown Soda Bread

Use 225g (8oz) plain, white flour and 225g (8oz) plain, wholemeal flour, and follow the recipe for white soda bread.

Scone Rounds (*without yeast*)

These are light textured scones which are quick and easy to prepare and bake. The variations make them suitable to serve with any meal to replace traditional bread. They also freeze well.

Ingredients

450g (1lb) self-raising flour
Pinch of salt
100g (4oz) butter or margarine
40–50g (1½–2oz) caster sugar
2 eggs, beaten
Approx 175ml (6fl oz) milk
  (preferably sour)

Sieve the flour and salt into a bowl. Add the butter or margarine and rub in until the mixture resembles fine breadcrumbs. Mix in the sugar. Make a well in the centre of the mixture and add the eggs. Add sufficient milk to mix to a soft dough. Turn out on to a floured surface, divide into two equal pieces and flatten out each one with your hand to a round about 2cm (¾in) thick.

Transfer to greased or floured baking sheets and mark each round deeply into eight wedges. Either leave plain or dredge with flour. Bake in a very hot oven, 230°C (450°F) mark 8, for 15–20

minutes, until well risen and browned. Turn on to a clean cloth on a wire rack, wrap up and leave to cool. Break into wedges as required.

Alternate Sweet Toppings

The rounds can be brushed with beaten egg or milk and, if liked, be sprinkled with one of the following before baking : demerara sugar, chopped shelled walnuts, cinnamon or mixed spice, crushed sugar lumps, etc.

Fruited Scone Rounds

Add to the rubbed in dry ingredients 100g (4oz) currants, raisins or sultanas ; or 100g (4oz) mixed dried fruit ; or the grated rind of 1 large orange or lemon ; or a mixture of fruit and 50g (2oz) mixed peel or chopped nuts.

Wholemeal Scone Rounds

Replace half the self-raising flour with brown self-raising flour or brown plain flour mixed with 7.5ml (1½ level tsp) baking powder, and follow the recipe for basic scone rounds.

Savoury Scone Rounds

Prepare the basic scone round mixture, omitting the sugar and adding any of the following to the dry ingredients : 75–100g (3–4oz) finely grated cheese ; or 30–45ml (2–3tbsp) freshly chopped herbs ; or 3–4 cloves crushed garlic or the equivalent of powdered garlic. Sprinkle the tops with flour, or grated cheese or rock salt, or brush with egg or milk.

Note Using cutters, or by cutting the dough into triangles or squares, the mixture can also be made into scone rounds of various sizes, ie 2.5cm (1in), 4cm (1½in), 5cm (2in), etc. Placed on a greased or floured baking sheet with the scones almost touching each other. Bake as for the basic scone rounds for 12–15 minutes. Cool on a wire rack wrapped in a clean cloth.

Further reading from David & Charles

GOOD FOOD GROWING GUIDE
Gardening and Living Nature's Way
John Bond and the Staff of 'Mother Earth'
A new-look growing guide to healthier and
happier living
241 × 148mm   illustrated

ECONOMY COOK BOOK
Mary Griffiths
A guide to how to cope with rising food and
housekeeping prices and still produce tasty
and nutritious meals
216 × 138mm

COST-EFFECTIVE SELF-SUFFICIENCY
Or The Middle-Class Peasant
Eve and Terence McLaughlin
A practical guide to self-sufficiency, proving
that life as 'middle-class peasants' is not only
viable but enormously enjoyable and satisfying
247 × 171mm   illustrated

EAT CHEAPLY AND WELL
Brenda Sanctuary
Rising food prices make this up-to-the-
minute book a must for today's housewives
216 × 138mm   illustrated

GROWPLAN VEGETABLE BOOK
A Month-by-Month Guide
Peter Peskett and Geoff Amos
A practical, easy-reference guide to growing
super vegetables, and fruit too, month by
month
250 × 200mm   illustrated

GROWING FOOD UNDER GLASS:
1001 Questions Answered
Adrienne and Peter Oldale
An indispensable guide to setting up and
maintaining every kind of glasshouse,
together with an A–Z rundown of the familiar
and unusual fruit and vegetables to be grown
210 × 148mm   illustrated

GROWING FRUIT:
1001 Questions Answered
Adrienne and Peter Oldale
Answers all the questions a novice might ask
about pests and diseases, choice of tree
shapes and varieties, and pruning techniques
210 × 148mm   illustrated

GROWING VEGETABLES:
1001 Questioned Answered
Adrienne and Peter Oldale
All you need to know about growing
vegetables in a simple question and answer
format
210 × 148mm   illustrated

**COMPLETE BOOK OF HERBS AND
SPICES (New edition)**
Claire Loewenfeld and Philippa Back
A comprehensive guide to every aspect of
herbs and spices—their history and traditions.
cultivation, uses in the kitchen, and health and
cosmetics
240 × 171mm   illustrated

COOK OUT
Frances Kitchin
For the cook on a caravanning or camping
holiday, Frances Kitchin provides the answers
to all the problems when cooking meals with
the minimum of facilities
210 × 132mm   illustrated

**British Library Cataloguing in
Publication Data**

Wadey, Rosemary
  Baking breads.—(Penny pinchers).
  1. Bread
  I. Title
  641.8′15   TX769

ISBN 0–7153–7535–0

Bread for cover illustration supplied by
Thomas of Bovey

First published 1978
Second impression 1978
Third impression 1978
© David & Charles Ltd 1978

Set in Univers
and printed in Great Britain
by Redwood Burn Limited
for David & Charles (Publishers) Limited
Brunel House   Newton Abbot   Devon

Published in the United States of America
by David & Charles Inc
North Pomfret   Vermont 05053   USA